Managing Bank
Capital

Published in association with:

Swiss Bank Corporation

SBC Warburg

A DIVISION OF SWISS BANK CORPORATION

Short Biography

Chris Matten is an Executive Director with Swiss Bank Corporation, based in Switzerland, where he heads the Corporate Controlling function. A chartered accountant, he spent six years in Japan, first with Price Waterhouse and later with UBS before moving to SBC. He returned to Europe in 1991, since when he has been helping SBC to build modern management information tools, initially in Capital Markets & Treasury – Risk Control and since April 1994 with a Group-wide focus. He is the author of several articles on risk and risk capital, and a regular speaker at conferences, most often on the subjects of capital allocation and disclosure of derivatives.

Managing Bank Capital:

Capital Allocation and Performance Measurement

Chris Matten

John Wiley & Sons

Chichester • New York • Brisbane • Toronto • Singapore

Published by John Wiley & Sons Ltd,
Baffins Lane, Chichester,
West Sussex PO19 1UD, England

National   01243 779777
International   (+44) 1243 779777

Reprinted December 1996, December 1997, September 1998

Notice

Datastream is a registered trade name, trademark and service mark of Datastream International Limited.

All data and graphs contained in this publication and which have been obtained from the information system of Datastream International Limited ("Datastream") are proprietary and confidential and may not be reproduced, republished, redistributed or resold without the written permission of Datastream.

Data in Datastream's information system have been compiled by Datastream in good faith from sources believed to be reliable, but no representation or warranty express or implied is made as to the accuracy, completeness or correctness of the data. Neither Datastream nor such other party who may be the owner of any information contained in the data accepts any liability whatsoever for any direct, indirect or consequential loss arising from any use of the data or its contents. All data obtained from the Datastream's system and contained in this publication are for the assistance of users but are not to be relied upon as authoritative or taken in substitution for the exercise of judgement or financial skill by users.

Library of Congress Cataloging-in-Publication Data

Matten, Chris.
    Managing bank capital : capital allocation and performance
measurement / Chris Matten.
        p.   cm.
    Includes bibliographical references and index.
    ISBN 0-471-96116-7
    1. Bank capital – Management.   2. Bank investments.   3. Asset
allocation.   4. Asset-liability management.   5. Risk management.
I. Title.
HG1616.C34M37   1996
332. 1'068'1–dc20   95–53023
                                                                CIP

British Library Cataloguing in Publication Data

A catalogue record for this book is available from the British Library

ISBN 0-471-96116-7

Typeset in 11/13pt Times by Saxon Graphics Ltd, Derby
Printed and bound in Great Britain by Biddles Ltd, Guildford and King's Lynn
This book is printed on acid-free paper responsibly manufactured from sustainable forestation, for which at least two trees are planted for each one used for paper production.

Contents

To Lusi, for putting the sun back into my life

Acknowledgements

There are many to thank in a work such as this, heavily dependent as it is on SBC internal research as well as academic papers; it would be impossible to list everyone who has been involved in this process, and I must therefore start by apologising to anyone whose contribution is not mentioned below.

My interest in capital allocation was sparked many years ago, when a small group of us sat down every couple of months and tried to solve the problems involved from first principles. We all had very busy schedules and precious little time for any research; the consequence was that our conversations had the excited feeling of travellers in an unexplored land. We have come a long way since then, but I wish to thank all of the members of that working group, and in particular Marco Suter, Mike Allen and Joe Doherty, for starting me off on this journey.

A very special vote of thanks has to go to Bob Gumerlock, who guided me not only professionally but also personally through a very difficult period in my life. Bob's influence underlines all of this book: the free reign he gave me to study the problem, the encouragement he gave me when I was feeling blocked, the lessons he gave me in statistical techniques and last but not least his enthusiastic support of this book project. Mentor, manager, friend: for all of these roles I am indebted to him.

Over the past two years, I have had the pleasure of working for Peter Wuffli, Chief Financial Officer of SBC—a pleasure which I hope will continue! I thank Peter for allowing me to write this book and to use SBC's knowledge base in doing so. But more importantly, I wish to thank him for subjecting my ideas to his critical review, and on at least one occasion for supplying a breakthrough insight at a truly critical moment.

There are many other colleagues whose contribution deserves to be honoured; thanks go to Richard Schneider for his support and ideas, to Hugh Parry for many long hours philosophising over a great deal of Swiss beer, and to Basil Miller for taking many of these ideas and putting them into practice (on occasion in excruciating detail!). I thank also my immediate colleagues Patrick Freymond and Andy Jacobs for doing much of the research and providing a sounding board for my ideas, and I must reserve a special mention for John Sandbach, who knows more about valuing banks than any sane person would wish to know.

Outside SBC, I wish to thank Lillian Chew, consulting editor at *Risk* magazine, whose own book project has been running parallel to mine, for encouraging me to write and for introducing me to John Wiley & Sons as publisher.

It is customary for an author to acknowledge the contribution of what we must call in this age of political correctness his/her 'significant other', and I have good reason to abide by this custom. My wife Lusi has been a tremendous help, and I am particularly grateful for her patience whilst I spent many a Sunday at home bashing away on the computer keyboard. Fortunately, we had a miserable spring in Switzerland (and the summer was not too hot, either), so this did not test her patience too hard. However, I think I might have to think twice before I allow some-one to talk me into writing another book!

Finally, indebted as I am to the many people who have supported me in this endeavour, I must take the full responsibility for what lies herein. Not only are any errors and omissions entirely at my door, I must also emphasise that the opinions expressed herein are mine alone, and do not necessarily reflect the opinions of my employer, Swiss Bank Corporation.

Introduction: Capital Allocation in Banking

Commenting on the way banks seem to be able to squander the capital invested in them, a financial journalist wrote recently: 'Giving capital to a bank is like giving a gallon of beer to a drunk. You know what will become of it, but you can't know which wall he will choose'.[1] This pungent reflection on the efficiency—or lack thereof—with which banks manage their capital goes a long way towards explaining the increasing interest in the subject of capital allocation seen in recent years.

Ever since General Motors pioneered modern cost accounting and capital allocation techniques back in the 1920s, the theory of capital allocation has been a standard part of any competent finance practitioner's toolkit—be he financial controller, corporate finance executive or management accountant. In their book *Relevance Lost*, Messrs Johnson and Kaplan[2] show how management accounting techniques have failed to really evolve much since then, with the last big step forward (the introduction of net present value techniques) coming as long ago as the 1950's. Unfortunately, what Johnson and Kaplan have to say about industrial companies is even more true of the financial sector, which was so heavily protected until the end of the 1970s that there was no need for anyone to worry about efficient allocation of resources. As the age of '3–6–3 banking' (borrow at 3%, lend at 6%, be on the golf course by 3 p.m.) came to an abrupt end, banks were forced to become competitive, and fast. Whilst some banks have risen admirably to this challenge, on the whole capital allocation and performance measurement skills in the banking industry still lag way behind those employed in manufacturing companies as well as in other branches of the service sector.

The specific problem in the case of banks comes in the unique form of their balance sheets—whereas an industrial company uses a mixture of debt and equity to provide operational finance (investment in plant and equipment as well as providing a sufficient level of working capital), a bank's source of finance (mainly customer deposits) cannot be seen as external funding of the business: it is part of the business itself. The problem is further complicated by the fact that banks are required to maintain levels of equity that they do not strictly need to finance their operations (even a heavily retail-oriented bank will typically have less than half of its equity invested in the physical assets of banking—branches, computer systems etc.); these requirements are imposed by the market (depositors will want to place their deposits in 'safe' banks, as is amply illustrated by the enormously high capital levels of private banks, which run very few risks compared to their retail or commercial banking brethren), or by regulations. Finally, banks may be either asset-driven (i.e. the majority of their business is in creating assets, such as loans, leaving a portion of the balance sheet for which the bank has to seek refinancing) or liability-driven (in which case the problem is where to invest the surplus funds).

For all these reasons, the textbook approach to capital allocation cannot be applied directly to banks. Whereas some banks and some consultants have (at least in their own words) created their own solutions to the problem, they have been remarkably coy about publishing the details. In some cases (notably Bankers Trust's RAROC system) there is clearly an understandable unwillingness to give away the crown jewels for free; in other cases, one suspects that the reluctance to spell out the exact details may be because there aren't any. This book is intended to fill this gap in the literature.

Those readers who are hoping to come across a single magic formula which Swiss Bank Corporations' alchemists have dreamed up will be disappointed, as such hopes rest on nothing more than perhaps the mediaeval roots of Basle University. There is no such magic formula. There are, however, a limited number of techniques which are suitable for making decisions in varying circumstances, and a number of other techniques which probably ought to be avoided except in unusual circumstances. This book looks at a variety of different techniques, and illustrates their uses. There are certain fundamental principles of finance, however, which are common to all of the good techniques, and the best advice to most banks is to pick two or three different measures, and test them for internal compatibility as well as for consistency with the fundamental principles, and with each other. The ultimate test is whether the approach taken is consistent with the enhancement of shareholder value, which is why there is a chapter dedicated entirely to this subject.

There are many different kinds of bank: retail, investment, private, merchant etc. This book is written from the perspective of a universal bank, which is involved in virtually all branches of the banking industry (this makes the problems of capital allocation particularly acute, as it is not easy to put the different businesses on a common measurement basis). It is hoped therefore that there will be parts of the book which will be of interest to all kinds of banks, although probably only the universal banks will find all of the book relevant to their situation.

It is one of the initial assertions of this book that the problem of efficient resource allocation faced by banks is a direct result of the increasing competitive pressures resulting from deregulation. Of course, some observers might point out that many large bank bail-outs have been observed in recent years, indicating that the 'market' is not being allowed to dictate as much as we might assert. Such large bail-outs (of virtually the entire Scandinavian banking industry, for example) have indeed been observed, and arose as a result of the importance of the banking industry to the economy in general, both as an intermediator of funds as well as the administrator of the payments system. However, this does not alter the fact that shareholders are more demanding, that the market is more competitive, and that it is in every bank's interest to improve its performance. There may still be a central banking safety net, but that is no excuse for falling off the high wire.

The stock market has taken a mixed view of the performance of banks over the past one and a half decades; in the USA, stock prices have broadly kept up with the overall market, with some significant volatility from year to year, as can be seen from Figure a.

The USA has—as in so many other areas—led the world in terms of the speed with which its banks (but perhaps not its savings and loans industry!) have grasped the nettle of competition, and the resulting improvement in profitability seems to be supported by the performance of banking stocks. In other parts of the world, banks have only recently been exposed to a competitive market, and the result has been a lack of pressure to improve returns, and thus a rather lacklustre performance in the eyes of the stock market (see Figure b, which shows the performance of continental European banking stocks).

This book attempts to address the issue of capital allocation from the perspective of improving performance—measured from both inside the bank as well as from outside. By improving the capital allocation

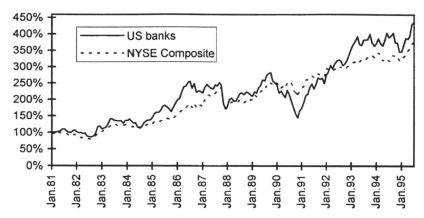

Figure a   Relative stock price performance 1981–1995: US banks
Source: Datastream

process—even simply by realising the need for one in the first place—it is argued that managers can improve returns earned on that capital.

Part One (Chapters 1 and 2), looks at the role of capital in general and establishes a definition of both its components and its function. The difference between *investment* and *allocation* of capital is also examined: a very crucial distinction which is often overlooked.

The structure of Part Two (Chapters 3 to 6) mirrors the development of capital allocation techniques, from regulatory capital models through to the various in-house approaches. All of these models have some measure of return divided by some measure of capital, and are covered by the generic term 'Return on Capital' (RoC). Chapter 3 first looks at the most basic capital allocation model—the regulatory requirements—and examines both its strengths and its limitations. This is followed in Chapter 4 by the internal counterpart of the regulatory approach—the 'asset-volatility' methodology most commonly encountered in the 'value-at-risk' (VAR) measurement system and the related risk-adjusted performance measures (RAPM—usually pronounced 'rap-em' in the trade). Chapter 5 then moves on to the derivation of a target return on capital and a basic bank-wide model for capital requirements. Finally, Chapter 6 examines an alternative to the asset-volatility approach: the earnings volatility model.

Part Three (Chapters 7 to 10), looks at the limitations of the RoC approach as a performance yardstick: firstly, at some of the practical, data-related problems, and the sophistication which needs to be built into

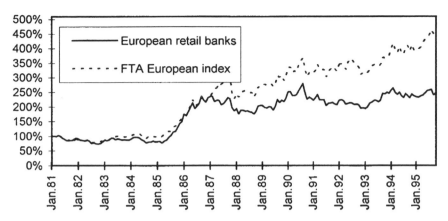

Figure b   Relative stock price performance 1981–1995: European banks
Source: Datastream

management accounts to overcome these. The difference between the internal management measurement of RoC and the stock market's perspective is examined in Chapter 8, which asks whether the stock market takes any notice of the existence of sophisticated capital allocation techniques. Our attention is then directed to a concept which is becoming more and more popular: shareholder value analysis (SVA) and the related economic value added (EVA), whilst the last chapter of the book is dedicated to the procedural and management aspects related to establishing a risk capital model.

A short word on nomenclature: there are no standard names for most of the techniques used in this book. Different banks and consulting firms have their own proprietary names; they may call a technique shown here by another name; they may use a name used here for a different technique. The author has chosen the labels used here as those which best seem to fit the different techniques, and hopes that this book will at least contribute to a more common language platform when such techniques are discussed at conferences etc. A rose by any other name may indeed smell as sweet, but it could get awfully confusing at the florist's!

Finally, a word on statistical techniques. Many of the developments in capital allocation rely on statistical techniques, some of which are quite sophisticated. Whereas a basic knowledge of statistics will assist the reader in understanding this book, it is not a prerequisite. Basic statistical techniques are explained in a way that the layman will understand—and apologies are offered to the statistician who may find the portrayal over-simplistic as a result. Wherever necessary, more detailed information on the statistical techniques employed is included as an appendix to the relevant chapter.

ENDNOTES

1. Christopher Fildes, writing in the *Spectator*, August 1995.
2. H. Thomas Johnson and R. Kaplan, *Relevance Lost: The Rise and Fall of Management Accounting*, Harvard Business School Press, 1987.

PART ONE
The Role and Definition
of Capital

1
The Role of Capital: Why are Banks Required to Hold Capital?

Why do banks hold such large amounts of capital? This may seem a very banal question, but the answer is not as obvious as one might at first imagine. However, before turning to the question of how much capital banks really need, and how to allocate it across different businesses or activities, a clear understanding of the exact definition and role of capital in the banking industry is required. A number of hypotheses are presented here to explain why it is that banks are capitalised at their present levels, looking at both the pressure from regulators as well as other influences. Brief case studies of three banks—Citibank, Lloyds Bank and Bankers Trust—illustrate both the importance and difficulty of maintaining adequate amounts of capital.

THE DEVELOPMENT OF CAPITAL STANDARDS FOR BANKS

Until the late 1970s, banks were in general highly regulated, and highly protected, entities; this protection was largely a result of the bitter memories of the Great Depression in the US as well as of the role which uncontrolled inflation (hyperinflation) played in the political developments in Europe during the 1930s. The activities banks were allowed to undertake were tightly restricted by national regulators, and in return banks were protected from competitive forces. The Bretton Woods agreement, established in the summer of 1944, put in place a system of exchange rate (and consequently interest rate) stability which ensured that banks had an easy time managing their exposures. At the same time, the strict control over the issue of banking licences also ensured that banks could operate as a cosy club without fear of take-over or turf incursion by outsiders. In many cases, this protection went as far as government-dictated interest rates on customer deposits, making it virtually impossible for banks to compete with each other in any meaningful way, even if they wanted to.

This cosy relationship was intended to ensure stability of the banking system, and it succeeded in its goals throughout the reconstruction and growth phases which followed the Second World War. The system held up well until the early 1970s, when the collapse of the Bretton Woods agreement led to a substantial increase in exchange and interest rate volatility. This sudden increase in uncertainty was in turn exacerbated (from the banks' point of view) by the gradual relaxation of exchange-control regulations. Central banks were left with only one effective way to implement monetary policy: by exercising their influence over the supply of money to banks, and therefore over interest rates.

The resulting strain on the banking system was enormous: banks were faced with an increasingly volatile environment, but at the same time had very inelastic pricing control over their assets and liabilities, which were still subject to both government regulation and protective cartel arrangements. The only solution was deregulation—or, in other words, exposing the banks to the cold wind of competition. The age of '3–6–3 banking' was over.

The result was somewhat predictable: an industry unaccustomed to competitive pressures became suddenly prone to excess, over-lending to Latin American governments, over-paying for stockbroking firms in London etc., as the all-out drive to come out in front of the pack dominated management's attention. The consequent erosion of capital started to alarm the regulators, as the spectre of large banking failures started to loom ever larger (particularly in Japan, where the surplus of yen awash in the system coupled with the most stringently controlled domestic banking industry in the G10 led to a massive expansion offshore, often at kamikaze prices which the western banks could —would not—match).

The only way to address this situation without increasing the competitive differences between countries was at the international level; a committee was thus set up under the auspices of the Bank for International Settlements in Basle to see what could be done. This committee, initially known as the Cooke Committee after its chairman, was subsequently renamed the Basle Committee on Banking Regulation and Supervisory Practices, and is today often referred to simply as the BIS. A detail often overlooked is that the Committee is not actually part of the BIS — it simply meets under the umbrella of the BIS, which also provides administrative support. The Committee consists of representatives of the central banks and supervisory authorities of the G10 countries,[1] and although its recommendations have no legal force, the governments of the G10 countries are morally bound by the nature of their respective countries' representation on the Committee to implement its recommendations in national law.

The Cooke Committee published its proposals for comment in December 1987, and the final agreed version, published in July 1988, is often referred to as the 'Basle Accord' or the '1988 Accord'.[2] This was a ground-breaking document, establishing a common minimum framework for calculating the capital adequacy of banks, which the member countries committed themselves to turn into national law by December 1992. By and large, the member countries dutifully complied, with a little bit of special pleading to protect national interests, of course (the Japanese banks, who were the primary target of the Accord, had difficulty complying and so special transitional arrangements were granted; the Japanese were also granted special rules relating to the valuing of their enormous stock holdings, which are not marked to market). Perhaps appropriately, given its host country status, the Accord was based very closely on the regulations which already existed in Switzerland.

We will return in Chapter 3 to the 1988 Accord's rules and methodology; for now, it is sufficient to say that the basic approach taken was to 'risk-weight' assets according to their riskiness (e.g. exposures to G10 governments were deemed to be risk-free and consequently assigned a risk weighting of 0%; claims on G10 banks were assigned a risk-weight of 20%, as these banks are covered by the capital requirements of the Accord; other banks and corporations generally attract a risk-weight of 100%); capital must be held at least equal to 8% of the sum of the risk-weighted assets. Off-balance sheet exposures such as guarantees and swaps are converted into asset-equivalents effectively by multiplying them by conversion factors, with two different methodologies being allowed for derivatives.

Much criticism has been levelled at the 'crude' nature of the 1988 Accord, but nobody can deny its success in both levelling the playing field, by bringing national practices into line, as well as improving the capital adequacy of banks. This is amply demonstrated by Table 1.1, which shows the ratio of capital to risk-weighted assets for a number of major banks in 1989 and 1993.

Table 1.1 Tier 1 ratios

	1989	1991	1993
Japan	4.10	4.64	5.15
France	n.a	4.82	5.88
Germany	n.a	n.a	5.27
UK	6.10	6.50	6.57
USA	4.23	5.13	7.69
Switzerland	n.a	7.77	8.04

Source: IBCA, EuraCD

The 1988 Accord addressed primarily the credit risks inherent in banks' activities; one of the consequences of the Accord was that banks looked for ways to generate earnings in ways which did not tie up regulatory capital. For example, the Accord does not distinguish between different kinds of private-sector customer: making a loan to Nestlé and to the corner shop carry the same risk weight. This made loans to poor credits relatively more attractive, hastening the departure of the high-quality loan customer which the process of securitisation had already started (why borrow money from a bank when you can get a much better price from the securities markets?). It also encouraged banks to take on new risks—such as market risk in a dealing operation—which are not reflected at all in the 1988 Accord.

To their credit, the Basle Committee was and is aware of these short-comings—the risk-weight on loans, for example, is intended as an average, and does not prevent banks from using a sliding scale internally to price loans properly. The issue of market risk is referred to in the 1988 Accord,[3] and the Committee (in the meantime renamed more simply the Basle Committee on Banking Supervision) has published proposals for extending the capital adequacy rules to the market risks taken on in the dealing function.[4] At the time of writing these proposals have yet to be finalised, and a lively and instructive dialogue has taken place between the industry on the one hand and the regulatory community on the other.[5]

However, many innovative banks have decided not to wait for a 'perfect' regulatory model and have developed their own models for allocating capital to individual transactions or businesses, and most of this book is dedicated to these techniques.

THE ROLE OF CAPITAL

Given the prominence and impact of the Basle Accord and subsequent proposals, one might turn to these in order to find an answer to the question 'why do banks have to hold capital?' This is not just an academic question: the more capital banks have to hold (in the form of equity), the more difficult it is to generate the return required by shareholders!

The introduction to the Basle Accord states that its objectives are twofold: firstly, to 'strengthen the soundness and stability of the international banking system' and, secondly, to 'diminish . . . an existing source of competitive inequality among international banks'.[6] The second aim is simply a reflection of the fact that, without global harmonisation, there will be competitive imbalances in the system, with different banks subject to different standards. This is important: as noted, the level of capital affects the return required by shareholders and a bank with a lower capital requirement would be able to price its products more keenly, as its threshold return would be lower. The first of the quoted goals gets close to what we are looking for: by forcing banks to hold a minimum capital level, there is less likelihood of bank failure, thus bringing greater stability to the system. Thus capital requirements can be said to have replaced the earlier system of regulated deposit rates, cartel agreements etc. which had protected the banks in the past.

The Basle Accord makes this 'buffer' role clear when discussing whether general loan provisions are to be included in the definition of capital. Such reserves are only admissible when they are not ascribed to particular assets: 'where, however, provisions have been created against identified losses . . . they are not freely available to meet unidentified losses which may subsequently arise elsewhere in the portfolio and do not possess an essential characteristic of capital'.[7] An essential element of capital is therefore its availability to absorb future, unidentified losses.

How big, then, should this buffer be? The Basle Accord introduces a target 8% capital ratio; however, this ratio is not based on any empirically derived formula, but was of necessity fashioned in the crucible of supranational political debate: the framework of the Basle Accord could just as easily be applied to a minimum capital threshold of 6%, or 10%, or any other number (remember that the Accord firstly calculates the risk-weighted asset equivalents, and then requires that capital be held at least equal to 8% of this amount).

The 1993 proposals on market risk are a little bit more forthcoming, in that they introduce the concept of a level of probability of loss. This is a very important concept, and must underline any discussion of the role of capital in a bank. For now, we will keep this concept at a very general level, but we will return to it in more detail in later chapters.

A first attempt at defining the role of capital in a bank would thus state that capital acts as a buffer against future, unidentified losses, thereby protecting depositors. This, however, is not enough, as any observer of bank 'runs' knows. A bank exists partly as an intermediary between savers and borrowers, pooling depositors' money and lending it out to those in need of credit. Thus only a small proportion of depositors' funds are available as cash at any point in time—if a large number of depositors try to withdraw funds at the same time, the bank may be unable to meet their demands, leading to rumours that the bank is 'bankrupt' and a subsequent panic as even more depositors turn up to try and rescue their deposits. This can happen to a perfectly healthy bank.[8] Thus the 'margin for error' for a deposit-taking bank must be somewhat larger than simply a cushion against 'normal' losses in any particular period: capital must be sufficient to cover even very improbable events, otherwise the bank will not be viewed as being sound. This perhaps explains the very high capital levels of private banks, which do not lend money to risky credits and do not trade for their own account, and thus do not require much in the way of capital to absorb losses, but whose customers still demand a very high level of perceived safety from the institution to which they entrust their (often very substantial) wealth.

A recent survey carried out by the *Nihon Keizai Shimbun*, Japan's leading financial daily, illustrated this point. The survey[9] reported that many housewives—typically the guardians of the family finances in Japan—were worried about potential bank failures, and 'half of the . . . respondents said that they would withdraw all of their funds if their bank were to report a loss.' Although losses are a very rare and severe event in Japan, due to the flexibility given by Japan's financial accounting standards to 'window dress' results, the implication of this quote is that if a bank reports a loss, it could be forced into bankruptcy by a mass withdrawal of deposits. The fact that a bank reports a loss does not necessarily mean that it is insolvent—it just has a lower capital buffer until the next profit can be used to repair the difference. But depositors may not agree with this analysis, and take fright. However, it should be noted that Sumitomo Bank, just two weeks after the survey was reported in the press, broke ranks with tradition and reported a loss for the 1994/95 financial year (the Japanese banks have otherwise been using a number of regulatory 'exemptions' to defer accounting in full for the problem loans incurred as

Japan's bubble economy collapsed). Unless it has gone unreported in the press, there has not been a run on Sumitomo.

Capital for banks cannot be compared with simple creditor protection for normal companies, which requires simply that the difference between assets and liabilities be positive. In the case of a bank, the capital base has to be sufficient to absorb even relatively improbable losses, and yet leave the bank able to operate at the same level of capacity—much of the value of a bank's activities is dependent on the bank being able to continue operations (a loan, for example, will realise its full value in terms of a positive interest margin only if the lender continues in existence long enough to collect all of the payments, unless he is able to transfer these rights to another party). We can therefore state that the *role of capital in a bank is to act as a buffer against future, unidentified, even relatively improbable losses, whilst still leaving the bank able to operate at the same level of capacity.*

THE DEFINITION OF CAPITAL

There are many different definitions of capital, starting from a very narrow 'equity plus stated reserves' through to something that encompasses subordinated debt (i.e. debt which ranks below all other creditors in the case of a winding up). The Basle Accord uses a two-tier concept, where Tier One consists of share capital and disclosed reserves, and Tier Two includes such items as 'hidden' reserves, unrealised gains on investment securities, and medium- to long-term subordinated debt.[10] The total of Tier Two capital is not allowed to exceed Tier One.

The 1993 proposals go even further, introducing a third category of capital (short-term subordinated debt) which can only be used to underpin market risk capital.

However, the focus of this book is on helping management maximise the return for shareholders, and therefore a more narrow definition of capital is relevant, i.e. shareholders' equity. Note that this may not quite be equal to published equity, as banks may hold 'hidden' reserves (these are created by either deliberately undervaluing assets such as securities holdings, or by over-valuing liabilities, e.g. by creating provisions which are not strictly necessary). The movements between these reserves and the P&L account were always hidden, in that they were lumped in with other items and not separately disclosed, and banks used these hidden reserves to smooth out some of their profit volatility by creating reserves in good years and releasing them in leaner years. However, the practice is now virtually outlawed in most G10 countries, at least for publicly quoted banks.

The techniques illustrated in this book all take equity as the definition of capital. However, a broader definition of capital can always be accommodated, simply by scaling up. Thus if a bank wishes to regard its subordinated debt as a substitute for capital, and if debt is 20% of the total capital, then a capital requirement of $100 can be thought of as $80 equity and $20 debt. The mix between debt and equity which a bank adopts will be driven by tax considerations as well as by local regulatory requirements.

In general, it is advisable for banks to try and use debt for at least a portion of their capital needs, as it is much more flexible: there is nothing more frustrating for managers who are trying to improve the share price performance than being left with a legacy of high equity and a lack of projects in which to invest it. Classic corporate finance theory states that, if management cannot find projects which earn at least the cost of equity, they should return the equity to the shareholders; this is much easier said than done in the case of banks. For example, in order to repay capital local rules may require that creditors' permission be obtained, and since every depositor is in effect a creditor of the bank, this may imply obtaining the permission of literally millions of creditors! However, holdings of own shares are now permitted to a degree in many countries, allowing banks to reduce their equity by buying back their own shares on the market.

If banks make full use of the allowable Tier 2 capital (remember that this cannot exceed Tier 1, so up to 50% of capital can be financed by such items as subordinated debt), this will at least give management the flexibility to reduce capital on maturity of the debt with no adverse consequences: if the capital is no longer required, then the bank can simply refrain from making any new debt issues. Where the bank is able to earn returns which are greater than the cost of capital, this excess will of course accrue entirely to the shareholders, which is another reason why banks should take as much advantage as possible of the capital leveraging allowed to them.[11]

HOW MUCH CAPITAL DOES A BANK REALLY NEED?

Most banks now hold equity which is in excess of the regulatory minimum (see Table 1.1). So why is it that banks now hold more? There are many theories put forward as to why this is: perhaps management, with a much better understanding of the risks the bank really faces, considers that the regulatory minimum is insufficient? Perhaps there are market forces which require this, such as pressure from rating agencies to maintain a certain excess in order to support a superior credit rating? Or perhaps it has happened almost by accident?

It is very difficult to comment on the first of these hypotheses, as the managers of banks are understandably reluctant to publish details of how much capital they think they really need—usually, they are happy to trumpet the excess over the regulatory minimum as some sort of achievement. This certainly may help to attract depositors, but the shareholders might not quite see it the same way, as it is their investment which is apparently lying idle.

Relationship between credit ratings and capital ratios

The evidence in support of the hypothesis that banks raise their capital ratios as a response to pressure from rating agencies is inconclusive. All bankers who have been involved with their organisation's contacts with rating agencies know that this is indeed a major topic of discussion, but the empirical evidence suggests that the link between capital ratios and credit ratings is not as strong as one might think.

Figure 1.1 shows the Tier 1 ratios and Moody's credit ratings for a selection of major international banks at selected points over the past few years. There is clearly no direct relationship between the two. Some of the outliers can perhaps be explained by special forces—the two points representing relatively high credit ratings (A) but low capital ratios (around 3%) relate to Banque Paribas, where factors such as implicit government guarantees and non-Tier 1 capital may play an important role (although Moody's state quite clearly that they concentrate on Tier 1 capital). There are also a number of banks with high capital ratios but low credit ratings—these are mainly large American banks which had recently built up strong capital ratios, but had yet to demonstrate that they had overcome their tendency to over-lend to problem sectors (such as Citibank), which might have given the rating agencies grounds for

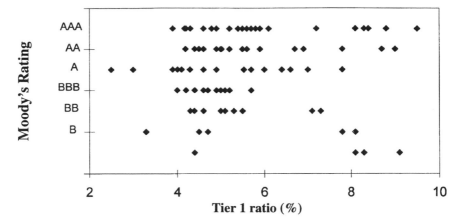

Figure 1.1   Credit ratings vs Tier One ratios: Moody's

extra caution. One must also bear in mind that these banks built up their
capital ratios very rapidly in the early 1990's, and there is an inevitable
time delay between the change in a bank's financial circumstances and
the corresponding change in its credit rating. Even deleting the outliers,
however, there is no statistical relationship between credit ratings and
capital in this sample.

Figure 1.2 repeats the analysis, this time using ratings from Standard
and Poors (S&P). The same core group of mainly American banks provides the grouping down in the bottom right-hand corner (high capital

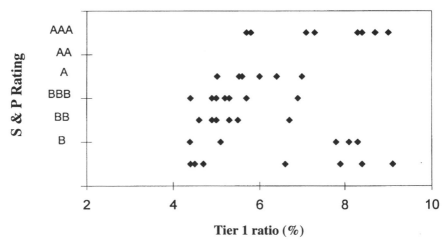

Figure 1.2   Credit ratings vs Tier One ratios: Standard & Poors

ratios but low credit ratings), but otherwise the data is slightly better grouped than in the case of Moody's (the sample is, however, not identical, as not all historical ratings were available from both agencies for all banks). The statistical relationship is stronger, but still very slight indeed. Interestingly, there were no banks in the sample with low capital ratios but high credit ratings.

The evidence is therefore not very conclusive, although at least in the case of S&P it seems that a negative causality can be ascertained: high capital ratios do not guarantee a good credit rating, but low capital ratios seem to correspond to a low credit rating.

High capital ratios as an historical accident

There is at least anecdotal evidence in support of the third hypothesis—that the current high capital ratios have arisen by accident. During the late 1980s, after the publication of the Basle Accord, banks were put under pressure by the regulators to improve their capital ratios. Some banks stated this openly as one of their main goals (Citibank is a prime example). As the banks increased their capital balances either by issuing new equity or by withholding dividends, the world economy entered recession, and the banks were faced with a falling off of loan demand. In addition, the process of disintermediation continued to lead to a reduction in the top-rated loan customers, as these turned more and more to the capital markets for their funding needs. Finally, at least at some banks, the increased awareness of the need to price risk properly into loan margins meant that the banks were less willing to lend to lower-rated customers. The result was an unforeseen increase in capital balances and reduction in capital needs. This is understandable, given the fact that banks were operating in a new environment, under new rules, and it was therefore very difficult to gauge the outcome of a given program. The boom in trading profits, particularly in 1993, was certainly better than anyone expected, and despite the rather more disappointing performance of 1994, it left banks sitting on more capital than they intended.

The anecdotal evidence is supported by the warnings which have recently been issued that banks are again under-pricing loans, presumably because they have nothing else in which to invest their surplus capital. Figure 1.3 has been taken from a recent BIS quarterly report,[12] and shows quite clearly that margins on large syndicated loans have recently been falling quite steeply.

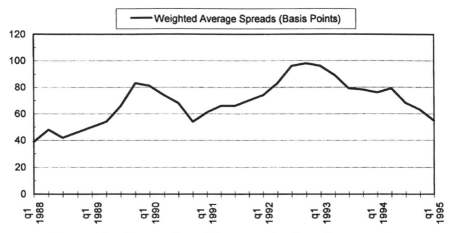

Figure 1.3 Average Spreads in International Syndicated Credits
Four-quarter moving average of spreads over LIBOR on USD credits
Source: BIS

This will almost certainly backfire: the experience of loan losses in the past — and agencies such as Moody's regularly publish bond default statistics which support this — indicate that the margin being demanded on these loans is insufficient to cover the credit risk being assumed. (The pricing of credit risk is an important component of any capital allocation scheme, and a technique to account for this is introduced in Chapter 7.)

Using the BIS statistics, the effective return which banks are earning on these credits can be estimated (see Table 1.2). Unfortunately, the BIS statistics do not split the OECD/non-OECD categories into types of borrowers, so it is assumed here that they are all corporates and thus subject

Table 1.2   Return on international syndicated credits

	Mix	Risk weight
OECD sovereigns	17%	0%
Other OECD	68%	8%
Non-OECD	15%	8%
Average		7%
Per $1 credit		
Capital requirement		0.07
Margin over LIBOR		0.0055
Return on capital		8.3%

to the full 100% risk weight (translates into an 8% capital requirement). This leaves a gross return of 0.55 cents (55 basis points) on a 7 cent capital requirement, or a return of around 8%. This may seem acceptable, but the cost of capital of most banks is probably much higher than 8%. Also, this is a gross return—before costs, before loan loss provisions etc. Indeed, a good benchmark for most banks is an annual loan loss provisioning requirement of around 30 to 50 basis points on the value of the portfolio—wiping out most of the margin on these syndicated credits! Whilst one can object that the banks may have a higher margin than 55 bp (as they can get sub-Libor funding, such as from customer deposits), that the assumption that all the non-sovereign credits take a full 100% risk-weight is too conservative, and that loan losses on this type of credit are not as high as the 30–50 bp average (which includes a lot of more risky retail credits etc.), the calculation highlights two important points which will be re-encountered several times in this book.

1. It is very important to work out the marginal cost of capital, including costs, likely credit losses etc., when pricing transactions. Here regulatory capital was used, but other measures may be equally useful, such as the risk capital concepts introduced in later chapters.
2. Many banks may simply be comparing the gross margin against an alternative investment in, say, government bonds, and concluding that the extra margin, even if below the cost of capital, is worth earning. This ignores the importance of the cost of capital to the bank, and will eventually detract from the overall value of the bank.

Further evidence that banks are currently over-capitalised comes from the USA.[13] According to the Federal Deposit Insurance Corporation, US banks raised some $31.7 billion in equity between 1991 and 1994—and this during a period of record profits! As a result, Tier One capital rose by 43% whilst assets increased only by 16%.

Case study: Citibank

The example of Citibank would seem to support the theory that banks' reaction to the 1988 Accord resulted in higher levels of capital than the banks intended to have (this is not intended as a harsh criticism of the management of these banks—they were in totally unfamiliar territory, trying to pull levers without any experience of what would happen when they were pulled).

In his 1990 letter to the shareholders, Chairman John Reed introduced a 'five point plan' to turn the bank around. This plan was to be completed over the next two years or so, and one of its components was . . . 'a multi-year capital plan that will position Citicorp as 'well-capitalised'. We believe this implies adding the equivalent of $4 billion–$5 billion to Tier 1 capital.' At the time, the bank had total Tier 1 capital of $8 billion, and a Tier 1 capital ratio of 3.2%. Since the 1988 Accord allows Tier 2 capital up to, but not in excess of, the Tier 1 amount, the bank was clearly below the minimum hurdle of 8% overall set by the Accord, with which banks had to comply by the end of 1992.

Two years later, the 'five point plan' was stated as successfully completed, and the annual report for 1992 states 'At the end of 1992, Citicorp's Tier 1 capital stood at $10.3 billion, up from $8.0 billion at the Plan's inception. Total regulatory capital increased $4.1 billion to over $20 billion . . . Citicorp's year-end ratio of Tier 1 capital to risk-adjusted assets was 4.9% and its total regulatory capital ratio (Tier 1 plus Tier 2) was 9.6%. Both ratios are ahead of our Plan targets . . . .' The increase had been achieved partly through operating efficiencies (leaving more retained profits to boost reserves), partly through reduction in the size of the balance sheet, and partly through the issue of preferred stock.

Note that the original plan target was *not* reached—this called for an increase in *Tier 1* capital by some $4–5 billion! So at some point somebody must have realised that this was unnecessary, and re-interpreted the goal in a more realistic way. In addition, the annual report goes on to say that the Plan's targets were exceeded. All of this suggests that Citicorp's management raised more capital than they probably thought necessary. Indeed, when stating that the five-point plan was completed, management made it clear that many of the goals would continue to be business priorities—but no further reference is made to the capital level.

At the end of 1993 we can see that Citicorp's Tier 1 ratio had shot ahead to 6.6%, and its total capital ratio was a massive 11.45%—against a regulatory requirement of only 8%. This increase was partly as a result of 1993's record results, but it is very interesting to note that Citicorp issued $675 million in cumulative preferred stock in 1993. If management had been perfectly happy with a Tier 1 ratio of 4.9% one year previously, then 6.6% must be way in excess of what they wanted, and it is not at all clear why further stock issues were made.

In the 1994 annual report, capital comes back into the limelight. The Chairman's letter states that '. . . our Tier 1 ratio is 7.8% . . . We will build capital ratios to our targeted 8% Tier 1, 12% total.' Why the bank needs this level of capital is not at all clear, and one might question whether the shareholders agree with this use of their money. However,

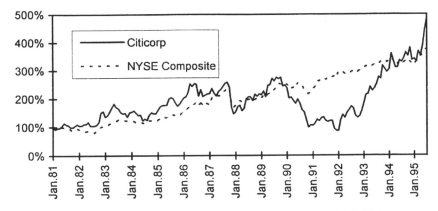

Figure 1.4   Relative stock price performance 1981–1995: Citicorp
Source: Datastream

the bank's results have been improving much faster than its capital balance, with the return on equity increasing pretty much constantly from 4.4% in 1990 to 21.4% in 1994.

The message so far from Citibank, then, is mixed: it first appears that the bank actually overshot its capital targets, but it then went on to increase those targets even more. Does this suggest that the management considers the regulatory capital limits to be inadequate? Given Citibank's experience in the LDC debt crisis in the early 1980s, the answer could be 'yes'. But what does this mean for the shareholders? Are they getting an optimum return?

We have to wait until some months after the 1994 annual report was published to get a clear answer. On 20 June 1995, Citibank announced that it would be launching a $3 billion share buy-back program. The *Financial Times* commented that, at the then-prevailing market prices, this would represent about 10% of the bank's equity—implying a reduction in the Tier 1 ratio to around 7%. It would seem that in the trade-off between building an adequate capital cushion and generating a decent return for shareholders, the bank had gone too far towards the former and realised that it needed to redress the balance. The stock rose immediately after the announcement, although not as dramatically as one might have expected. As Figure 1.4 shows, the stock price of the holding company, Citicorp, has underperformed the market for much of the last five years, but has recently caught up the lost ground as return on equity improved.

Case study: Lloyds Bank

Lloyds Bank is often quoted as the prime example of the benefits of focusing on return on capital rather than more traditional banking measures (such as balance sheet size), and certainly the performance of the stock is something of which the bank's management can be proud (see Figure 1.5).

The Chief Executive of Lloyds, Brian Pitman, changed the focus of his management to generating a satisfactory return on equity even before the Basle Committee issued the 1988 Accord on capital adequacy requirements, and it is probably fair to say that Lloyds was one of only a very few banks which realised the importance of generating a decent return for shareholders before the Accord was issued. The results speak for themselves: the stock price has outperformed the broad UK market index by a factor of more than two over the last 14 years; dividend growth has been spectacular at around 14% compound growth per annum over the past nine years, and the book return on equity (net profit divided by book value of equity) is often around 20%. And all this despite actually reporting a loss twice in the last ten years (1987 and 1989)!

Surprisingly, the bank achieved this without pushing its capital ratios to the limit: the Tier 1 ratio was 7.8% at the end of 1994, and the total capital ratio was a very comfortable 12.8%. Only once over the past ten years did the bank get close to the regulatory minimum (8.5% in 1990). How did Lloyds manage to reconcile high returns with a comfortable equity base?

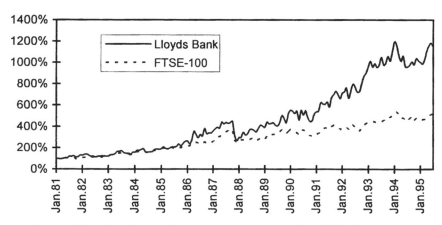

Figure 1.5   Relative stock price performance 1981–1995: Lloyds Bank
Source: Datastream

The answer lies in the bank's then unique focus on businesses which generate superior returns: businesses which were profitable, but not making a sufficiently high return on equity, were deliberately shunned at a time when competitor banks were running around acquiring assets that in some cases were not even profitable, in the mistaken belief that size and market share would count in the pending battle for dominance and even survival. Lloyds, the smallest of the 'Big 4' British clearing banks, deliberately shunned the mainstream: in the words of Brian Pitman's 1990 letter to shareholders '. . . our aim is to be the best, not the biggest . . . Our goal for return on equity is 18 per cent or more'.

In the case of Citibank, we saw that a key factor is to find the right level of capital: too little, and the bank faced a liquidity crisis; too much, and it was impossible to provide a decent return on equity. The example of Lloyds adds a second lesson: given a certain level of capital, it is important to be ruthless in investing only in businesses which generate superior returns (the basic point of any capital allocation process is to ensure that capital goes where it can work hardest). As of 1993, Lloyds was proudly trumpeting the fact that it had not asked its shareholders for more cash since 1976, and had been able to increase the dividend for 26 consecutive years.

Case study: Bankers Trust

Bankers Trust, too, is an institution which has been justly proud of its return on equity: despite losses in 1987 and 1989 (note the parallel to Lloyds), the bank has often produced returns in excess of 20% (measured as the book return on equity). The Tier 1 ratio was at 9% at the end of 1994, up from 7.7% at the end of 1992, and the total capital ratio was a very high 14.8%. In many respects, the returns earned and the capital base are very similar to those of Lloyds Bank.

However, the stock price performance of Bankers Trust has not been so spectacular as at Lloyds, although BT's stock too out-performed the index for much of the 1980s. As Figure 1.6 shows, the stock price has on several occasions given back the advances made and has fallen back to the level of the market as a whole. This happened in 1987, in 1989 and again in 1994, coinciding with the losses made mainly in the trading businesses in those years.

Bankers Trust is well known for its RAROC system of allocating risk capital (the RAROC concept and its many imitators is examined in Chapter 6), a system which the bank started to introduce in the late

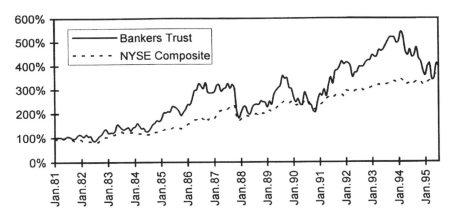

Figure 1.6   Relative stock price performance 1981–1995: Bankers Trust
Source: Datastream

1970s—in other words, long before the Basle Committee established an international capital framework. One would therefore expect Bankers Trust to be one of the top performers in the banking sector, given that (together with Lloyds) it was one of the very few banks which realised the importance of efficient capital allocation at such an early stage. The stock price performance shows that this has not been the case.

Part of the reason for this is the stronger emphasis on trading in Bankers Trust, whereas Lloyds is primarily a retail/commercial bank. Since the trading business is perceived as more volatile than traditional banking activities, shareholders require higher returns—in order to achieve the required yield on the stock investment, the market will lower the value of a stock if the earnings generated are not high enough. (Incidentally, this perception of trading as a more volatile business is not really based on a fair observation: the trading profits are marked-to-market (see Chapter 7), whereas the earnings on the credit business are spread over the tenor of the underlying transactions. At the same time, banks have many ways to smooth the impact of loan loss provisions over the years.)

But there is probably more to the story than just the higher required yield: after all, Lloyds also made losses in 1987 and 1989, and its earnings are probably nearly as volatile as those of BT. The average return on equity produced by BT has been a very respectable 22%, which should have been more than enough to compensate the shareholders for the level of risk being taken. It would seem that a sophisticated capital allocation methodology on its own is not enough, if shareholders believe that there are substantial, additional risks which are not being picked up. Some banking analysts have commented on the apparent conundrum, and have concluded that the severe reputational loss which BT suffered in 1994 in the wake of various headline derivatives 'disasters' (Procter & Gamble, Gibson Greetings etc.) proves that the market was right all along. The argument runs along the lines: 'if profits look too good to be true, that is probably because they are (too good to be true)!', and the market saw its scepticism vindicated.

The Bankers Trust example teaches us a third lesson to the two we have already learned: it is not enough to have a sophisticated capital allocation system in place if the market believes that there are hidden or systemic business risks which are not being considered in the process—the system must be translated into consistent and sustainable long-term superior returns.

THE DRIVERS OF CAPITAL LEVELS

In summary, then, there is no magic formula to determine the appropriate level of capital for any bank. Management must weigh up the following factors:

1. The level of capital which the credit rating agencies think is consistent with a given credit rating (either maintaining the current rating or achieving a certain target rating). No agency is going to give a firm commitment to a particular rating based solely on a particular capital ratio alone, but to the extent that it is a relevant factor, indications can be obtained through discussions with the agencies at the occasion of the normal analysts' visit.
2. The level of capital which the management of the bank thinks is appropriate, supported by an internal assessment of the capital at risk.
3. The regulatory minimum, as predicted by business plans, over the normal planning horizon. A margin for error needs to be built into this plan, as a regulatory capital shortfall can have very serious consequences.

Against these must be set the target return which management wishes to achieve. This will be driven by the market's expectations of returns—exceeding the market's expectations will result in an increase in shareholder value, whereas failing to meet those expectations will result in a destruction of value. The higher the amount of capital which a bank maintains, the higher the profit it will have to earn in order to make the target return.

MAKING THE MOST OF YOUR CAPITAL

Does efficient capital allocation work? A bank can surely optimise the relationship between return and capital by either of two means: increasing the amount of return earned per dollar of capital, or decreasing the amount of capital required per dollar of return. This focus on return is nothing revolutionary, but has been surprisingly absent from the boardrooms of most banks, at least until recently. During the period of deregulation during the 1980s, the main focus of the banks was to increase their size, usually measured as the volume of assets on the balance sheet. The typical goals given to a loan officer, for example, were: increase market share (asset growth), and increase the interest earnings (P&L growth). The link between the two was a misguided attempt to pay some attention to the need to increase the return if the size of the balance sheet was to grow. What actually happened was an ill-advised battle for market share, often for lower-quality loans—as these borrowers had to pay a higher interest margin to compensate for the lower credit quality, the twin goals of asset growth and earnings growth were met. Unfortunately, the increased margins at this end of the market were insufficient to cover the increase in the credit risk premium (to meet expected losses in the future) giving a very misleading picture of performance.

The evidence from those banks who concentrated on return on capital rather than growth is mixed—whereas in some cases this was clearly reflected in the form of superior stock price performance in other cases this was not so clear-cut.

However, one must conclude that sensible allocation of anything which acts as a business constraint—and there is no doubt that the need to earn a decent return on capital whilst at the same time maintaining certain minimum capital levels means that capital is a major business constraint—must be superior to an approach which leaves this to chance. Even using the regulatory capital model as a base will produce superior returns to a strategy based on pure balance sheet growth, as it uses a measure of *risk*, since regulatory capital is based on risk-weighted assets rather than unadjusted assets. However unsophisticated the risk adjustment is, some risk adjustment is usually better than no risk adjustment.

Finally, sophisticated capital allocation systems on their own will not automatically translate into superior performance, but, unfortunately, banks do not have much choice: poor capital allocation on the other hand will undoubtedly translate into inferior performance as an expensive resource gets wasted.

ENDNOTES

1. The G10 actually consists of 11 countries (Belgium, Canada, France, Germany, Italy, Japan, Netherlands, Sweden, Switzerland, the United Kingdom and the United States). Luxembourg—presumably because of its importance as a banking 'safe haven'—is also represented on the Basle Committee.

2. Committee on Banking Regulations and Supervisory Practices, *International Convergence of Capital Measurement and Capital Standards*, Basle, July 1988.

3. 'The framework in this document is mainly directed towards . . . credit risk . . . but other risks, notably interest rate risk and the investment risk on securities, need to be taken into account. . . . The Committee is examining possible approaches in relation to these risks' *ibid*, §8.

4. Proposals issued by the Basle Committee in April 1995, published as a set of separate documents.

5. The comments submitted by the various banking associations of the member countries are all illuminating, as is the response by the International Swaps and Derivatives Association. The only response to have been formally published was that of the Institute of International Finance, another industry body, which published its comments in October 1993 *(A response to the 1993 Basle Committeee Consultative Proposals*, IIF, Washington). See also *Risk* magazine, September 1993 pp. 72–91.

6. *International Convergence of Capital Measurement and Capital Standards*, §3.

7. *Ibid*, §18.

8. A few years ago, this apparently happened in Hong Kong. Unfounded rumours started to circulate about Standard Chartered Bank, an otherwise perfectly healthy bank, and customers rushed to pull their deposits. Fortunately, the bank's main office is situated right next to the main office of the HongKong Shanghai Bank, which is normally its main competitor, but which fully understood the consequences of a banking panic in the colony and gave Standard Chartered its full support by freeing up a virtually unlimited credit line. Thus customers walked out of the front door of Standard Chartered carrying their cash, and then deposited it next door with HongKong Shanghai Bank—which then shipped the cash out of the back door back into the tills of its neighbour! Eventually, customers realised that Standard Chartered seemed to have unlimited cash, and the panic abated. The next day, the cash flowed the other way as customers put their money back into Standard Chartered.

9. As reported in the *Financial Times* on 10 January 1995.

10. See *International Convergence of Capital Measurement and Standards*, Part I and Annex 1, for a full definition of the allowed components.

11. The purists will point to the famous proposition of Franco Modigliani and Merton Miller, whose work showed that, in theory, the overall weighted average cost of capital should remain unchanged regardless of the extent of leverage. However, even the authors then conceded that taxes distort this,

as the interest on debt is tax deductible for the borrower, whereas dividend payments are not. It is anyway very questionnable whether the theory would apply to banks: these already have enormous liabilities (customer deposits etc.) and the issue of a little bit more debt is unlikely to have an adverse influence on the rates required by either debtholders or depositors.

12. *International Banking and Financial Market Developments*, Band for International Settlements, Basle, May 1995.

13. The statistics quoted in this paragraph come from an article ('Loan arrangers ride again') in the *Economist*, 25 February 1995.

2
Introduction to Capital Allocation Techniques: How do Banks Invest Their Capital? And how do they Measure the Return on That Capital?

It is one of the contentions of this book that the managements of many banks have often failed to appreciate the subtlety of these questions, and this failure has been at least partly responsible for the generally poor stock price performance of banks over the past decade or so. At the root of the problem lies a confusion between the *allocation* of capital to particular businesses, and the *investment* of capital as a cash resource.

This confusion is natural enough when we consider the backward state of management information systems (MIS) in most banks. It is ironic that an industry which prides itself on its state-of-the-art technology and highly qualified staff should have such a poor basis for understanding its businesses. In part, this is due to the sudden change in the banking environment discussed in the previous chapter—any industry would have had difficulty keeping its MIS up to date during such a period of tumultuous change. In part, it is due to the nature of the products which a bank produces: whereas in most industries, the input and output of goods and services are measured in terms of money, in a bank it is money itself which forms much of the input and output. Finally, it is partly due to the fact that, during the headlong rush into new activities, most of the technology resource budget was absorbed by ever newer and smarter dealing rooms, leaving very little for the less glamorous issue of controlling and information systems.

Whilst banks were active in an essentially homogeneous business—

the taking of deposits and granting of loans—it made sense to regard the individual branch as the organisational unit which equated to a profit centre. A branch that was unable to find enough loans in which to invest its deposits had to lend the funds to another branch or even another bank, at market rates; likewise a branch that could not raise enough funds to finance all of its loans had to resort to the inter-bank market to fill the gap. It was therefore very easy to monitor the performance of each branch, as each was a separate unit with its own books and records, and at the same time the need to fill any asset or liability overhangs through interest-bearing loans or deposits at market rates ensured that there were no hidden subsidies.

Each branch was—and often still is—entrusted with a portion of the bank's capital to invest. The amount allocated to each branch (the juxta-position of 'invest' and 'allocate' here is deliberate) was usually depen-dent on the overall size of the branch's balance sheet, unless the branch was located in another country and perhaps subject to different regula-tions. 'Return on Capital' (RoC—some measure of profit divided by capital invested) became the logical measurement benchmark of profit centre (i.e. branch) performance.

This use of RoC as a performance measure becomes difficult—if not impossible—when banks start to engage in multiple, heterogeneous activities. Firstly, these activities may not be directly comparable with each other, unless some method is found to allocate capital in a truly risk-adjusted way. If capital is driven mainly by the size of the balance sheet, then any off-balance-sheet activities (such as guarantees or—under some accounting standards—derivatives) will appear to be using no capital at all, giving rise to an infinite RoC. Allocating capital on a risk-adjusted basis, be it the regulatory model or some internal model, goes a long way to solving this particular problem.

Secondly, the division of a bank into branches and businesses will almost certainly be on different axes. Unless the bank stipulates that each of its branches or subsidiaries is dedicated to a single business line, the true organisation of the bank will have a matrix format, as illustrated in Figure 2.1.

If the businesses are the primary organisational unit—as is often the case in today's functionally driven hierarchies—then the primary capital allocation must be to businesses, and not to branches, and the measure-ment of performance must be on some version of RoC by business, not by branch. However, local regulations, tax optimisation considerations or other constraints will undoubtedly play a role in the determination of

	Branch 1	Branch 2	Branch 3	Branch 4
Business 1	X	X		X
Business 2	X		X	
Business 3		X	X	X
Business 4		X		
Business 5	X		X	

Figure 2.1   Business/location matrix

how much physical capital is paid into a branch or subsidiary. At the same time, the globalisation of trading books may also mean that risks are being taken in one branch whilst revenues are being booked in another. Remember that our definition of capital is as a cushion against potential losses, and therefore we must conclude that the amount of capital held in a particular branch may bear little or no relation to the capital being put at risk by the activities carried out within that branch.

The narrow definition of RoC—profit divided by capital physically invested in a branch—no longer serves its original purpose as a measure of performance at the profit-centre level, and we therefore need to distinguish between the *investment* of the bank's capital, and the *allocation* of capital to businesses.

THE INVESTMENT OF CAPITAL

The expression 'investment' of a bank's capital refers to the process whereby the cash raised through issue of equity, the retention of profits etc. is physically invested in assets of a particular character.

This issue is given particular piquancy by the need for a bank to manage its interest-rate sensitivity. The values of most of the assets and liabilities of a bank—and many of its off-balance-sheet transactions as well—are very susceptible to changes in the level of interest rates. These interest rates do not always move in parallel: the yield curve prevailing at any point in time indicates the level of interest rates for transactions with different maturities—the maturity for these purposes being the point in time at which the interest rate is renegotiated or the transaction expires. (In practice, these numbers have to be adjusted to take account of intermediate cash flows, and a measure called the adjusted duration is most commonly used. This is an important point if you are an asset and liability manager or an interest-rate trader, but it is not essential for an understanding of the issues discussed here). The nasty thing about yield curves is that interest rates at different points on the curve do not move in parallel: an increase of 50 basis points in the 1-year rate does not mean an increase of 50 basis points in the 10-year rate. Thus a bank which is funding long-term loans out of short-term borrowings is incurring enormous interest rate risk, as illustrated in Figure 2.2.

In this simple illustration, the bank has priced loans at point B (9-year loans), and has financed these by borrowing short-term (point A). The bank may believe it has locked in a positive margin (the difference between point B and point A). However, if by the time the borrowings come to be repriced the yield curve has shifted (dotted line), then the bank will have to roll-over its borrowings at a higher rate (point A'), resulting in a reduced margin of B − A'. If, on maturity, the assets which were priced at B are replaced by equivalent assets, the bank will have an even lower margin of B' − A'.

This is very relevant when capital is invested in a branch, as that branch can use the capital as 'free funds' i.e. it does not have to pay interest on them. It can therefore use those funds to finance its business assets. It now has an interest-rate sensitive asset (e.g. a 10-year loan) and a non-interest-rate sensitive liability (capital). Effectively, the bank has invested its capital directly into 10-year assets. The choice of period over which a bank wishes to invest its capital can have a very material influence on the earnings of the bank.

Consider for example Bank A, which does not have any guidelines as to how its capital should be invested. If capital makes up 8% of the loans on the balance sheet, then each loan is effectively financed 92% by borrowings and 8% by non-interest-bearing capital. Table 2.1 shows the

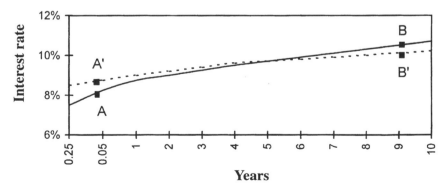

Figure 2.2   Pricing assets and liabilities of different points on the yield curve

interest-rate sensitivities which arise if these loans are made for 5 years when the 5-year rate is at 10% (we assume that the loans pay interest yearly).

Note that, as interest rates fall, the value of the assets rises (Bank A is earning 10% on something that, if entered into at the new level of interest rates, would only be yielding 9%). The value of the liabilities also rises—a loss to the bank—as it is now borrowing at 10% when it could be borrowing at 9%. The opposite happens when interest rates rise. The value of the capital remains unchanged—it is not interest-rate sensitive. In this case, the capital has been effectively invested at the 5-year rate.

Now consider Bank B. This Bank enters into exactly the same transactions, but forces its businesses to match-fund all assets and liabilities, and invests all of its capital in 30-year Treasury bonds. Let us also assume that the 30-year bond yield does *not* change in tandem with the five-year rate (in practice, the long end of the yield curve is indeed much less volatile than the short end), but that the bond yield remains unchanged. The resulting sensitivity to changing interest rates is shown in Table 2.2.

Since the bond value remains unchanged, and the interest-rate sensitive items are fully matched, the bank's value does not change with shifts in the 5-year rate. Of course, Bank B is still exposed to interest rate risk, but this risk is now related to the 30-year bond yield, and has nothing to do with the sensitivity of the loan activity. Note that we can still say that bank B has underpinned the loan business with 8% capital—it has simply decoupled the issue of underpinning (allocation) from the issue of asset and liability management (investment).

To make the examples clear, we have made the borrowing and lending rates equal. In practice, the bank will be able to lend at a higher rate than it must pay on its borrowings, as it will be charging a 'spread' for

Table 2.1 Value per $100 at different interest rates

	9%	10%	11%
Value of loans	103.89	100.00	96.30
Value of borrowings	−95.58	−92.00	−88.60
Net assets	8.31	8.00	7.70
Value of capital	8.00	8.00	8.00
Revaluation of net assets	0.31	0.00	−0.30
Net worth	8.31	8.00	7.70

Table 2.2 Value per $100 at different interest rates

	9%	10%	11%
Value of loans	103.89	100.00	96.30
Value of borrowings	−103.89	−100.00	−96.30
Value of bond	8.00	8.00	8.00
Net assets	8.00	8.00	8.00
Value of capital	8.00	8.00	8.00
Net worth	8.00	8.00	8.00

its services, and to cover credit risk. The borrowing and lending rates will be separated by this margin, but are still related to the same point in the yield curve, and will thus move in tandem. By this means, the bank is able to lock in a margin over the life of the transaction and has isolated itself from interest rate risk in this business, as illustrated in Figure 2.3. It does, of course, still carry the *credit* risk on the loan.

We can thus see that the choice of investment for the bank's capital can have a marked impact on the bank's earnings and value. It is therefore imperative that the physical investment of capital be clearly distinguished from the allocation of capital to businesses. If the individual businesses are allowed to decide how to invest the capital, they are most likely to use it as 'free' funding of their respective products, with little regard to the interest rate exposure of the bank as a whole. Unless great care is taken to charge the opportunity cost of funds this can even distort the apparent profitability of these businesses (i.e. if the bank has decided that capital is to be invested in 30-year Treasuries, then the cost to any

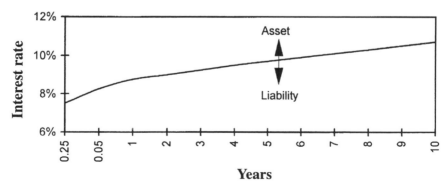

Figure 2.3 Pricing assets and liabilities off the same point on the yield curve

business of using capital as 'free' funds should be the yield on 30-year Treasuries).

At Swiss Bank Corporation, only the interest rate trading area is allowed to take a position on interest rates. All interest rate risk is transferred to this business, leaving all other businesses exposed only to whatever risks are relevant to those businesses (analogous to our example of bank B above). However, the interest rate business is charged for the capital invested based on the bank's desired investment horizon. Thus if the traders invest the capital over the bank's stated investment horizon, they will be treated as having no position. A different investment pattern is legitimate, but automatically gives rise to a trading exposure as they are 'borrowing' over the official investment horizon and lending over another. This exposure must be taken within approved trading limits, and gives rise to an allocation of (risk-based) capital—there is no free lunch.

INVESTMENT IN OTHER NON-INTEREST-SENSITIVE ITEMS

Capital is of course not the only non-interest-rate-sensitive item—in particular, the bank may have a substantial amount of real estate (branch network) and computer investment on its balance sheet. It is not intended here to digress into a thesis on asset and liability management, which would require a book on its own, but senior management needs to be aware of the other non-interest-sensitive items, as investing all of the capital of the bank into 30-year Treasuries may not quite achieve the desired effect: management needs to consider the net position of all non-interest-rate-sensitive items. At SBC, we treat all of these as having the same interest rate sensitivity as our desired investment horizon, which achieves the same effect as investing the net position over that horizon. It has the advantage over the net approach, however, of allowing the refinancing cost associated with, say, the retail branch network, to be charged as a cost to the retail banking business.

The important thing to note here is that there is no prohibition on businesses using the bank's capital as a source of refinancing: as long as the businesses are charged with the appropriate yield for the bank's desired investment horizon, and the interest rate 'mismatch' or 'gapping' analysis treats this as a loan by Treasury to the business at the appropriate duration, the same desired effect is achieved.

THE ALLOCATION OF CAPITAL

The term 'allocation' of capital refers to the process whereby a notional or pro forma calculation of the amount of capital underpinning a business is made. This is distinct from the investment of capital, in that no actual cash investment takes place. The notional calculation can be driven by any one of a number of different methods, as examined later in this book, and is often used as the basis of performance measurement.

Of course, the sum total of the amount of capital allocated should not exceed the total capital available (and invested); it may, however, be less. Indeed, it is very important that management does not just allocate out the total capital on a pro-rata or other such basis, as this provides no incentive for businesses to maximise their return. Instead, management must define a methodology under which capital will be imputed to businesses and then allocate the appropriate amount of capital. Any excess capital is not attributable to the businesses, but is a 'spare' corporate resource which earns only the risk-free rate of return (assuming that the bank has indeed invested all of its capital in a risk-free asset).

One way of envisaging this process is to think of the capital invested in risk-free bonds, which are then held as collateral to underpin the various activities of the bank. Seen in this light, the bank is like a hedge fund. Indeed, given that banks are able to obtain substantial leverage by borrowing more than ten times their capital in order to make risky investments (loans as well as trading positions in a range of financial instruments), it can be argued that banks have a lot more in common with hedge funds than many bank managers would like to admit.

The *investment* of the capital is in a long-term riskless asset, whereas the *allocation* of the capital is in risky businesses. This view is consistent with the decoupling of the interest rate risk in the investment from the interest rate risk in the business activities demonstrated in the previous section. However, it gives rise to a further area of confusion: the difference between net and gross returns.

NET VERSUS GROSS RoC

If all of our assets and liabilities are treated as if they were externally financed or invested, then the sum of the earnings of all component businesses is going to be less than the earnings of the bank as a whole, as the capital is a non-interest bearing source of funds. Consider a simplified bank (Bank C), with assets (loans) of $1000, earning 6%, and $900 of deposits on which the bank pays 4%. The bank's operating costs are $14, and the capital invested is $100 (see Table 2.3).

This bank can be broken into two businesses (loans and deposits), and a Treasury function; Table 2.4 shows the results of each business based on an opportunity cost of funds basis.

The example assumes that the mid-market rate is 5%, and that the internal funds transfer pricing system uses this rate (see Chapter 7 for a more detailed discussion of funds transfer pricing). The loan business therefore has to refinance its $1000 of loans at 5%—this is offset with Treasury (the reversal to interest expense in the Treasury column). The deposits business has to invest its $900 of deposits with Treasury, likewise at the mid-market rate. Some capital has been allocated to deposits, also based on an opportunity cost principle: at the very least, the bank would have to invest these in the inter-bank market, so one could calculate the theoretical capital charge attaching to $900 of inter-bank deposits (the numbers here are illustrative only).

The loan business achieves an RoC of 5%, deposits 10% and the Treasury 40%. The return to the Treasury arises because the Treasury has effectively invested all of the capital of the bank at 5%, but is only imputed with holding the surplus $10 of capital which is not required by the two businesses. The returns shown by the two businesses are on a *net* basis; that is, they express the return achieved in excess of the risk free rate (in this case, equal to the mid-market refinancing rate).

Table 2.5 examines the figures on the assumption that the capital allocated to each of the businesses had actually been available to that business as 'free funds'.

Note that the loan business now only has to refinance $940 ($1000 less $60 of capital) at 5%. The deposits business is able to reinvest $930 ($900 plus $30 of capital) at 5%. The RoC of each has gone up from 5% to 10% and from 10% to 15%, respectively. The difference between this return and the previous one is exactly equal to the mid-market funding rate, i.e. 5%. We call this the *gross* method of calculating RoC.

Table 2.3 Bank C. Simplified P&L account

Interest income	(6% × 1000)	60
Interest expense	(4% × 900)	−36
Net interest margin		24
Operating expenses		−14
Net profit		10
Return on capital		10%

Table 2.4 Management accounts on a fully funded basis

	Loans	Deposits	Treasury	Total bank
Interest income	60	45	−45	60
Interest expense	−50	−36	50	−36
Net interest margin	10	9	5	24
Operating expenses	−7	−6	−1	−14
Net profit	3	3	4	10
Capital	60	30	10	100
Return on capital	5%	10%	40%	10%

The choice of adopting the net or gross method of RoC is simply one of management preference; the advantages of one are the same as the disadvantages of the other, as can be seen in Table 2.6 opposite. At SBC, we actually use both: we report the P&L account for each business on a net basis, but add back the theoretical interest on capital allocated to express RoC as a gross number. We prefer gross as a measurement yardstick, as it is more intuitive (if I lend you $10 and you return to me $12 one year later, I consider you to have earned a 20% return on my money—I do not normally deduct the opportunity cost of funding the $10 for one year). It is also more useful when comparing businesses with external benchmarks, as the return earned by an independent corporation includes the opportunity gain derived from the fact that it can partly fund itself out of interest-free equity. However, we calculate the net profit on a net basis because it puts a business requiring financing and capital (e.g. loans) on the same basis as a business requiring only capital (such as a swaps portfolio) and one generating funds but not necessarily requiring any capital

Table 2.5 Management accounts on a 'free funds' basis

	Loans	Deposits	Treasury	Total bank
Interest income	60	46.5	−46.5	60
Interest expense	− 47	− 36	47	− 36
Net interest margin	13	10.5	0.5	24
Operating expenses	− 7	− 6	− 1	− 14
Net profit	6	4.5	− 0.5	10
Capital	60	30	10	100
Return on capital	10%	15%	− 5%	10%

(such as deposits). A further disadvantage of the gross method is that the measurement of revenue is dependent on the amount of capital allocated—using more than one measure of capital implies more than one measure of revenue, making the P&L account very confusing.

The 'net' and 'gross' methods are applicable to all capital allocation techniques: having allocated an amount of capital to a business (remember the difference between allocation and investment), we can decide whether to impute an investment of the capital (gross method) or not (net method). When looking at the performance of units with paid-in capital (be it branch capital or equity capital) it is very important to ensure that appropriate adjustments are made to reflect the fact that paid-in capital may not be equal to the allocated (imputed) capital in the business, giving a return number which is neither net nor gross. At SBC, we do this by charging interest in our management accounts against paid-in capital, which puts all results onto a net basis. Then, as noted above, restating returns on a gross basis requires no more than a simple calculation.

If calculated properly (Chapter 7 looks at some of the things that can be overlooked), the following rule will always hold true:

$$net\ RoC + risk\text{-}free\ rate = gross\ RoC$$

Table 2.6   'Net' vs 'Gross' method for determining RoC

	'Net' Method	'Gross' Method
Advantages	● Easy to calculate funds transfer pricing based on opportunity cost of funds (no need to calculate capital requirement as part of funds transfer pricing calculation) ● Useful if more than one RoC measure to be driven off same P&L	● Intuitive for most users
Disadvantages	● Not intuitively obvious	● Requires inclusion of capital calculation in funds transfer pricing system ● Need for multiple P&Ls if more than one RoC measure used

PART TWO
Capital Allocation in
Practice

3

Regulatory Capital: Is it Really as Irrelevant as Everybody Says?

The term 'regulatory capital' applies to the minimum capital requirements which banks are required to hold. Chapter 1 showed how these requirements have developed, and the role of the Basle Committee on Banking Supervision in this process. This chapter will examine the question whether regulatory capital has any role to play in internal capital allocation, or whether it should simply be regarded as a constraint at the level of the bank as a whole.

The international guidelines established by the Basle Accord have been applied broadly consistently within the G10 countries, but some differences may exist. For example, a major difference between the rules applying in the European Union (the Capital Adequacy Directive—CAD) and the Basle guidelines is that the EU did not want to wait for agreement on the capital required to underpin market risks and developed its own rules. In the meantime, the Basle Committee has issued its own guidelines for market risk, which differ from the CAD rules when the specifics of the calculations are looked at. However, this chapter will look at regulatory capital in a general sense and will thus always refer to the Basle guidelines. Whereas individual regulatory environments may diverge from these, the broad framework remains the same: it is not within the scope of this book to provide a point-by-point analysis of the differences between, say, the CAD and the Basle proposals. Bank managers will of course need to be familiar with their own regime.

OVERVIEW OF REGULATORY CAPITAL FRAMEWORK

(Readers familiar with the current international capital adequacy framework may wish to skip this section.)

1988 Accord

The framework introduced by the Basle Committee in 1988 has been adopted as the underlying structure of all bank capital adequacy regulations throughout the G10, and in some non-G10 countries as well. The Basle Committee left numerous places in the framework where local regulators could choose the appropriate percentage or select between alternative approaches, and thus there will be differences between these local rules even if they are fully 'Basle-compatible'. However, the structure is always the same.

Firstly, a bank sorts its assets according to certain risk weightings. These broadly reflect the riskiness of the assets and, as the banking industry in the 1980's was heavily biased towards the credit business (remember that the Accord was introduced to strengthen banks in the wake of the Latin American debt crisis), these risk weightings broadly reflect creditworthiness. Whilst loans to corporations carry a 100% risk weight, loans to banks within the OECD will carry a lower risk weight (usually 20%) and loans to national borrowers may take an even lower risk weight. Credits to OECD governments are deemed to be risk-free (cynically, one can suggest that by this means these governments ensured that they would always be able to fund their spending deficits by issuing bonds to the banks and keeping short-term interest rates low enough to make this attractive).

Contingent assets such as guarantees, letters of credit etc. are firstly converted into asset-equivalents by multiplying them by a percentage which broadly reflects the likelihood of the conversion into actual exposure.

Derivatives can be converted into credit equivalents by one of two methods. Under the 'original exposure method', the simpler of the two, the notional amount of the derivatives contracts is multiplied by a percentage chosen according to the original maturity of the contract and the type of underlying instrument. This results in an amount which is intended to reflect the likely maximum actual value of the contract during its life.

Table 3.1   Conversion of derivatives under 'original exposure' method

Maturity	Interest rate contracts	Exchange rate contracts
Less than 1 year	0.5%	2.0%
>1 year and <2 years	1.0%	5.0%
For each additional year	1.0%	3.0%
Example: currency swap with notional amount $100 million, maturity 3 years		
Credit equivalent = $100m × (5%+3%) = $8 000 000		

In the example shown in Table 3.1, the $8 million credit equivalent would then be multiplied by the appropriate risk weight (depending on whether the counterparty is a corporation, an OECD bank, etc.) to arrive at the risk-weighted asset.

The second method for derivatives, the 'current exposure method', takes the current market value of the derivatives contracts and adds to that an 'add-on', again expressed as a percentage of the notional amount, to reflect the potential maximum increase in value until maturity. The add-ons are based on the remaining time to maturity, not the original length of the contract. Only the positive market values (i.e. those contracts where the counterparty would have to pay the bank money if the contract were to be terminated) are included; negative market values are ignored, even if they are with the same counterparty. However, the 'add-on' part of the computation is applied to all contracts. The current market value of all contracts which have a positive value, ignoring any contracts with a negative value, is known as 'Gross Replacement Value' or GRV. An example is given in Table 3.2.

The $7 million and $250 thousand credit equivalents shown in Table 3.2 would again be multiplied by the risk weights appropriate for the respective counterparties. However, reflecting the fact that the average credit quality of a derivatives portfolio is usually much higher than that of a loan portfolio, the Basle Committee reduced the counterparty risk weight for corporations to 50% for this section of a bank's exposure.

The result of all these adjustments is to produce what are known as 'risk-weighted assets', which are simply summed. For example, assume that contract (1) in Table 3.2 was with an OECD bank (risk weight 20%) and contract (2) with a corporation (50%). In addition, there is a $20 million portfolio of corporate credits and $15 million of OECD government debt. Finally, the bank has issued a $5 million standby credit facility with

Table 3.2   Conversion of derivatives under 'current exposure' method

| | Add-ons | |
| | Interest-rate | Exchange-rate |
Residual maturity	contracts	contracts
Less than 1 year	nil	1.0%
More than 1 year	0.5%	5.0%

Example:
(1) currency swap with notional amount $100 million, maturity 3 years, current market value + $2 m
(2) interest rate swap with notional amount $50 million, maturity 2 years, current market value –$2 m

Total GRV (contract (1) only)	$2 000 000
Add-on on contract (1) – $100 m × 5%	5 000 000
Credit Equivalent on (1)	$7 000 000
Add-on on contract (2) – $50 m × 0.5%	250 000
Credit Equivalent on (2)	$250 000

a corporate customer, with a maturity of more than one year (this is converted according to the Basle Accord at 50% of its face value). Table 3.3 shows the calculation of the total risk-weighted assets.

The sum of the risk-weighted assets is compared with the available capital. The available capital (Tier 1 and Tier 2) must be equal to at least 8% of the sum of the risk-weighted assets: in the above example, total capital must exceed $1.74 million (8% of $21.77 million). Tier 1 comprises mainly shareholders' funds (equity plus disclosed reserves); Tier 2 includes such items as preferred stock and convertible debt, plus subordinated debt if it meets certain criteria (the debt must have a minimum

Table 3.3   Calculation of risk-weighted assets ($ thousands)

	Credit equivalent	Counterparty risk weight	Risk-weighted assets
Swap contract (1)	7000	20%	1400
Swap contract (2)	250	50%	125
Loan portfolio	20 000	100%	20 000
Govt. debt	15 000	0%	0
Standby facilities (5m × 50%)	250	100%	250
Total risk-weighted assets			$21 775

original maturity of at least 5 years, and cannot exceed 50% of the Tier 1 capital). A further restriction is that Tier 2 capital cannot exceed Tier 1.

Another way of expressing the same thing is to say that a corporate loan has to be supported by 8% regulatory capital (100% risk weighting), and a credit to an OECD bank with 1.6% (assuming 20% risk weighting etc.) Practitioners therefore often refer to an '8% capital requirement' or a '1.6% capital requirement'.

A major criticism raised against the Basle Accord is the lack of differentiation: all corporate credits take a capital charge of 8%, for example, regardless of the quality of the borrower. Thus a loan to Nestlé and the overdraft run up by the newsagent on the corner have identical capital charges (we will return to this point later in this chapter).

The Basle Accord has in the meantime been amended and proposals exist for further amendments. These amendments broadly reflect netting and market risk.

Netting

The amendments to reflect netting were promulgated in 1993 and finalised in 1994, with some further revisions added in April 1995. Netting refers to the process whereby a legally binding arrangement ensures that the claims and obligations against the same counterparty can be set off against each other. In the absence of this kind of legally enforceable arrangement, the liquidators of a bankrupt company can press for all amounts due to that company to be collected, whereas any amounts owed go into the pool of general creditors, who might receive only a portion of the amount lent by them. For example, imagine a bank has entered into two swap transactions with a company, one of which has a positive value of $100 to the bank and the other a negative value of $80, and the company then goes into liquidation. The derivatives transactions will automatically terminate early, and the bank would have to pay over the $80. At some point in the future, the bank might receive some of the $100 owing, depending on how much value the liquidators are able to realise. If the dividend to creditors is only 50 cents in the dollar, the bank will receive only $50 in return: what seemed to have a positive value of $20 ($100 less $80) turns into a negative value of $30—a loss of $50 overall. Under a netting agreement, the bank would be able to offset the $80 owed against the $100 owing, leaving only $20 outstanding. If the payout is again 50 cents, the bank will recover $10, giving an overall loss of only $10.

The revisions to the capital adequacy rules stipulate tough requirements which must be met for banks to be able to claim the benefit of netting when calculating their risk-weighted assets (to ensure legal enforceability). The bank must use the 'current exposure method' (as one needs to know the actual amount owing at the time of the calculation). A revised table of add-ons is then applied (empirical and theoretical arguments were submitted by the banking industry to show that the maximum potential value of the netted contracts is less volatile than that of non-netted exposures). At the same time, the Basle Committee expanded the add-on matrix to include other product classes; this revised matrix is shown in Table 3.4.

As before, banks calculate the value of their contracts, using the netted value ('net replacement value' or NRV) for those counterparties where netting agreements exist and meet the minimum requirements, and the GRV for the rest. The add-ons are again calculated on the basis of the notional amount, but are then multiplied by a formula which reflects the fact the potential change in value (which is what add-ons are supposed to capture) of a netted portfolio are less extreme than one where there is no netting. An example is shown in Table 3.5.

A complication with the add-on reduction shown in Table 3.5 is the fact that the net/gross ratio is a portfolio measure, but the risk weightings depend on the individual counterparty. Probably the easiest solution is to sort the portfolio into sub-portfolios for each risk-weight, and then perform the calculation separately for each (the paper published by the Basle Committee in April 1995 allows calculation of NGR at either counterparty-by-counterparty level or at an aggregate level).

Market risk

As banks have moved more and more away from the traditional credit business into new businesses such as investment banking, they have

Table 3.4   Revised table of add-ons

Maturity	Interest-rate contracts	Exchange-rate contracts	Equity contracts	Precious-metals contracts	Other commodities contracts
Less than 1 year	0.0%	1.0%	6.0%	7.0%	10.0%
> 1 year and < 5 years	0.5%	5.0%	8.0%	7.0%	12.0%
More than 5 years	1.5%	7.5%	10.0%	8.0%	15.0%

(Note that gold is treated as an exchange-rate instrument, not a precious metals instrument).

Table 3.5 Reduction of add-ons as a result of netting

The total add-ons are calculated on the notional amount of the contracts, and the sum is then multiplied by the following formula:

$$0.4 + (0.6 \times NGR)$$

where the NGR is the ratio of the replacement value after netting to the replacement value before netting ('net/gross ratio')

Example
The total add-ons amount to $600 million. The replacement value after taking netting into account is $1.5 billion, and $2.0 billion before taking netting into account (NGR = 0.75)

		$ millions
Replacement value:		$1500
Add-ons:	$(600 \times 0.4) + (600 \times 0.6 \times 0.75)$	$510
Total credit equivalent:		$2010

---

become more exposed to other risks, chiefly market risk. This refers to the sensitivity of the bank's proprietary trading positions to changes in the overall levels of financial markets. Of course, banks were always exposed in particular to interest rate risk, but the difficulties in producing a standard measure and the relative lack of importance of this risk compared to credit risk led the Basle Committee to leave it out of the original Accord. In April 1993, the Committee moved to plug this gap by introducing proposals for an additional market-risk capital requirement. The proposals however cover only the explicit trading book of the bank: the 'mismatch' in interest-rate sensitivities held on the traditional banking book is excluded. This is not because it is not a real risk, but because it is very difficult to arrive at common measurement standards (calculating the interest-rate sensitivity of some banking products—such as mortgages—is not so straightforward as one may believe!).

The 1993 proposals are long and only for the technically minded; space does not allow too much detail here, but a summary of the overall framework is required (a broad understanding of the concepts introduced here will be useful when looking at 'value-at-risk' approaches in Chapter 4).

In general, the proposals require breaking out the exposures to different risk classes (interest rates, equities and foreign exchange), and then multiplying these by sensitivity factors. For equities, this requires working out the net position in each stock in each market (i.e. offsetting long and short spot and forward positions as well as option positions, converted at their delta equivalents).[1] This gives the net exposure to each stock, which is multiplied by a risk-sensitivity factor of 8%. Market risk professionals would call this the 'specific' risk in equities. This charge replaces the 1988 Accord's requirement of 10% on common stock, and in many senses they are similar—the stock-specific component reflects negative information about the issuer, which can be seen as a kind of creditworthiness indicator.

However, stocks are also influenced by the overall movement of the stock market, which can give rise to profits or losses for the bank. The net position in each market is taken by summing all of the individual stock positions (after offsetting spot, forwards and options, as above), and offsetting long positions against short positions. The result is the net exposure to the market as a whole, which is multiplied by a sensitivity factor: the Committee again proposed 8%. Table 3.6 illustrates the calculation.

Note that for each separate capital computation it does not matter whether the position is long or short—the absolute net position in each stock and in the market is what counts. This is because market risk is two-sided: long positions lose money in falling markets, whereas short positions lose in rising markets. The capital calculations assume only that the market moves in whichever direction is adverse. Thus in the example

Table 3.6 Example calculation of equity market risk capital under the 1993 proposals

Stock	Position		Value
GM stock	Spot	Long 100 shares	5000
(mkt price $50)	Forward	Short 50 shares	−2500
	Calls	Short options on 140 shares	
		(delta 0.5)	−3500
	Net position in GM		−1000
IBM stock	Spot	Long 100 shares	9000
(mkt price $90)	Puts	Long options on 200 shares	
		(delta 0.4)	−7200
	Net position in IBM		1800
Net position in US stock market			800
Specific risk capital	GM	1000 × 8%	80
	IBM	1800 × 8%	144
General risk capital		800 × 8%	64
Total market risk capital			288

in Table 3.6, the market is assumed to go up in the case of the GM stock, but down for the IBM stock and for the market overall.

A similar process is carried out for interest-rate positions. Again, there is a specific risk charge against bonds (replacing the old credit-risk charge in the 1988 Accord), and then all positions are slotted into a number of different time bands to reflect their positions on the yield curve. Longs and shorts in each time band can be largely offset against each other, and there is some offset allowed between the time bands. And all this separately for each major currency.

In foreign exchange, there is no specific risk charge. Various treatments are allowed, but basically the requirement is to work out the net position in each currency (again after offsetting spot, forwards and options) and then to multiply it by 8% (this seems to be the magic number in capital adequacy rules).

The banking industry was very critical of the proposals, and the criticisms can be broadly summarised under two statistical concepts which are important to market-risk professionals (these same concepts will be encountered again in the following chapters in the context of risk capital): confidence intervals/holding periods, and correlations.

Firstly, the industry criticised the fact that, for example, all equity markets are deemed to show a potential loss of 8%. The statistically minded will express this as a problem of confidence intervals and holding periods (but do not worry if you are not—yet—familiar with these). In plain language, the assumption is that all equity markets are equally likely to rise or fall by an equal amount. But it does not require a market risk professional to observe that $100 invested in a well-developed stock market like the USA is nowhere near as risky as the same $100 invested in, say, India or Taiwan. This lack of differentiation can be corrected by using statistical models which estimate the potential moves of different markets at the same level of probability, based on their movements in the past. Thus rather than applying a broad 8%, different levels could be set for different markets. In many senses, this is the same criticism which is levied at the 8% on corporate credits in the 1988 Accord. The result of a lack of differentiation would be to motivate traders to take positions in risky markets at the expense of less risky ones.

The second criticism relates to the concept of correlation. All bankers understand this, at least intuitively: it is otherwise expressed as the concept of diversification, or 'not putting all of your eggs into one basket'. $100 lent to each of 10 different companies is less risky than $1000 lent just to one counterparty (assuming they all have the same credit rating at the outset, of course). The Basle proposals were again not sufficiently differentiated here—equity markets are in many cases historically correlated, and a short position in German stock is a better hedge against a long position in Swiss stocks than no hedge at all. Likewise, there may be correlations between different interest rates and different currencies which were not picked up by the proposals.

The Basle Committee thus issued revised proposals in April 1995 which reflected many of these criticisms. After a short comment period (until July 1995), the Basle Committee will probably produce a new Accord, for implementation probably by the end of 1996 or in 1997. Under these revised proposals, banks can basically be split into two classes. Those banks which have risk-management models which do many of the statistical things referred to in the previous paragraphs can use these models to estimate their market-risk capital. These models can differentiate between the potential moves of different markets (the proposals include requirements as to how long the observation period must be to derive these statistics, and the confidence intervals to be assumed when calculating the market-risk capital). Correlations within market-risk factors (e.g. between two different stock markets) are allowed, but not across risk factors (i.e. no offsetting between equities, interest rates and foreign exchange).

The second class of banks will be those whose supervisors are not satisfied that internal models exist or that these meet the necessary requirements. These banks will be forced to calculate capital based on the crude methodology introduced in the 1993 proposals—for any banks running significant market risks, this has the added benefit from the supervisors' perspective in motivating banks to install proper risk-management systems.

ASSET-VOLATILITY-BASED APPROACHES

There is one common theme running through all of the Basle proposals: the underlying idea is to estimate the potential loss to the bank caused by adverse changes in the value of its assets (or trading positions). This approach is described generically as an 'asset-volatility-based' approach to risk capital (the term 'asset' is used rather loosely here—a short position in stocks would not be described by most accountants as an asset, but the term here means anything which has an expected positive value for the bank). Under this approach, the asset is first converted into a standard measure of sensitivity to a loss in value (credit risk or market risk), and the resulting standardised exposure is multiplied by the potential change in the sensitivity factor to produce a theoretical loss in value which has to be matched with capital, as illustrated in Figure 3.1.

Asset (incl. market risk position, contingent asset etc)	X	Conversion into standardised measure of exposure to risk factor	X	Potential adverse movement in risk factor	=	Potential Loss in Value

Figure 3.1   The Asset-Volatility-Based Approach

The various in-house versions of the same approach are examined in the next chapter — indeed, it will be seen that many bank capital allocation models are simply refined versions of the regulatory model. As the regulatory model covers more risk classes, and becomes more refined in its coverage, a gradual convergence of the in-house and regulatory view of capital adequacy calculations can be observed. The very use of internal models to produce market-risk capital calculations for regulatory purposes bears witness to this gradual convergence of the two approaches, as the same in-house models may often be used to provide risk capital calculations for the bank's management.

REGULATORY CAPITAL AS A BUSINESS CONSTRAINT

It has been argued that regulatory capital is a meaningless measure—it is a regulatory constraint, but it cannot be used to allocate capital within the bank or to measure returns. This argument is a *non sequitur*: whilst regulatory capital is indeed in many cases not the most optimal yardstick to allocate capital within a bank, this does not mean that it can be ignored. An example at the margin illustrates the point. A bank can choose between two transactions, both of which have the same expected profits and, in the bank's view, are equally risky. However, the regulatory requirement is higher on transaction A than on transaction B. It is clear that the bank will choose transaction B, as it leaves more regulatory capital available for other investments.

The argument against regulatory capital is not so much that it is irrelevant, but that—unadjusted—it is not a good measure for efficient capital allocation within the bank. For example, the regulatory capital requirement on corporate loans translates to 8%—but this is regardless of the quality of the borrower or the tenor of the loan. However, raising this criticism is to misrepresent the intentions of the regulators who set these standards: the 8% charge is meant as an *average*, based on a conservative view of the likely components of the typical loan portfolio, taking into account diversification across borrowers, across branches and regions etc. When the 8% requirement is seen in this light, one can see that it should be reasonably easy to build an internal capital model, differentiated by tenor and credit rating, such that the average capital charge on the portfolio is equal to the 8% regulatory requirement. Thus loans to high-quality borrowers would attract an internal capital allocation of, say, 2%, whilst loans to the poorer-quality borrowers might require much more than 8%.

However, there is a potential problem with this approach. Given that loan spreads in the market may not properly reflect the bank's own view of the riskiness of a loan, distortions may appear in the potential returns. For example, the bank might calculate that a loan to an AA-rated borrower requires 2% capital, whilst that to a B-rated borrower requires 10%. If the spreads available in the market on the AA-rated loans are more than 20% of the spreads available on B-rated loans, the result will be an incentive to push loans to AA-rated borrowers at the expense of the B-rated clients.

(per $100)	AA-rated	B-rated
Internal capital requirement	2	10
Spread	0.50	2.00
Return on capital	25%	20%

A loan officer who tries to increase the mix of higher-rated business will use up capital (based on the table used internally) at $2 per $100 in such loans, despite the fact that the regulatory requirement increases at the rate of $8 per $100. He could thus end up using more regulatory capital than the bank has available.

Alternatively, the spreads on higher-rated loans could be lower than that implied by the capital model:

(per $100)	AA-rated	B-rated
Internal capital requirement	2	10
Spread	0.40	2.50
Return on capital	20%	25%

In this case, the loan officer will try to slant the portfolio towards the B-rated clients, which generate an apparently higher return. The result will be that he runs out of capital allocated to him (based on the internal model) before he actually uses up the regulatory capital available to the bank. The result would again be a sub-optimal allocation of capital, as any spare capital available to the bank is likely to be invested in risk-free assets such as government bonds, earning a return which is below the cost of capital of the bank.

This imbalance between internal and external models makes it very difficult for the internal model to be simply a more accurate version of the regulatory model, with higher levels of granularity. This is because any internal model which is set to equal the regulatory model at the portfolio level will move out of balance with the regulatory model as soon as the portfolio mix changes. It is probably sufficient only where the bank in question has a relatively stable portfolio mix (but then one can question why such a model is needed at all—if the bank cannot do anything to influence its business mix, it does not need a capital allocation model!).

This is an example of how imposition of a performance measurement can change the nature of what is being measured in an unpredictable fashion, and with negative consequences. The loan officer in our first example is justifiably trying to maximise what he has been told is the proper return, but with the result that the bank as a whole runs over its regulatory capital limit. In the second case, the bank fails to allocate all of the available capital and thus produces sub-optimal returns.

Some commentators have argued that regulatory capital is irrelevant, as risk (or 'economic') capital is always greater. The underlying observation for this argument is the fact that banks generally hold more capital than the regulations require them to. If this is the case, these commentators argue, it must be because management's own assessment of the capital required is greater than the regulatory capital. If this is true, then it is correct that regulatory capital is irrelevant, as the economic or risk capital model will always end up in a higher capital number. Whilst it is possible to show individual transactions where the regulatory capital requirement is higher than any internal risk capital number, taken as a whole, the argument maintains, the reverse would seem to be true.

Unfortunately, this argument is based on a fallacy: namely, that management deliberately sets internal capital requirements as higher than the regulatory model, implying that the regulators are not sufficiently conservative. There are at least four reasons why this would appear to be a fallacy.

Firstly, one can question why, if this were so, did banks not hold higher levels of capital prior to the issuance of tighter regulations in the wake of the 1988 Accord? It could be that banks just did not understand enough at the time, but one cannot deny the impact of the 1988 Accord on the level of capital held by banks. The statistics already seen in Chapter 1 show that the implementation of the Accord led to a marked increase in capital adequacy over the following years.

Secondly, there are very few banks in the world today which have risk-based capital allocation processes. This assertion is supported for example by a 1993 study by Salomon Brothers,[2] which concluded that . . . 'most firms have relied on regulatory . . . capital to drive their capital allocation process . . . only a handful of banks among the roughly 50 that we interviewed actually have installed a common, bankwide language that enables risk and reward to be evaluated across the product range.' The wide interest shown in conferences on capital allocation and the number of consultancy firms offering advice in this area also bear witness to this lack of sophistication in the industry. And yet virtually all major banks have capital which is in excess of their regulatory capital requirements (witness the improvement in capital ratios referred to in the previous paragraph). How can the internal measure of risk capital be higher than the regulatory measure if there is no internal measure?

Thirdly, as will be shown in Chapters 5 and 6, risk capital when measured on an 'earnings-at-risk' basis is *not* necessarily greater than the regulatory capital requirement, and may often be lower.

Finally, the evidence—anecdotal as it is—presented in Chapter 1 suggests that banks' apparent over-capitalisation is more accidental than deliberate, as seen in the example of Citibank.

This suggests that banks are in fact *forced* to be highly capitalised in an attempt to ensure compliance with regulatory standards—and that regulatory capital is a real business constraint and is therefore relevant in the capital allocation process.

However, the 'one size fits all' basis of regulatory capital itself cannot guarantee optimal capital allocation (witness the standard 8% on commercial loans, which does not differentiate between borrowers of different quality), and thus a need for a supplementary measure of capital arises.

MODELLING IN REGULATORY CAPITAL

Regulatory capital needs to be factored into the model, but without making it the sole constraint; there are several ways of doing this, two of which are illustrated below. Later chapters will provide models for determining the internal capital requirement—for now, these are simply referred to as 'economic capital'.

Imagine a single corporate credit, amounting to $100, earning a net margin of 1% (for the sake of the examples here, ignore whether this should be revenue, contribution after deducting direct costs, of whatever—it does not affect the points made in the examples). The capital requirement is 8% and the return on regulatory capital is therefore 12.5% ($1 divided by $8). Management consider that the true riskiness of this credit is closer to $2 (the 'economic' capital).

Treat regulatory capital as a cost of doing business

Under this approach, management will charge an appropriate cost of capital to the business. Assuming a risk-free rate of 5%, this gives a return of:

$$\frac{\text{earnings} - \text{cost of reg. capital}}{\text{risk capital}} = \frac{1-(8\times0.05)}{2} = \frac{0.6}{2} = 30\%$$

The problem with this approach is that it does not put any ceiling on the amount of regulatory capital utilised—as long as the business manager can earn returns which are sufficiently greater than the capital charge, he can go on adding more and more business. The regulatory capital can however be costed in at the cost of capital (say: 10%) rather than the risk-free rate, or at an even higher hurdle rate:

$$\frac{\text{earnings} - \text{cost of reg. capital}}{\text{risk capital}} = \frac{1-(8\times0.10)}{2} = \frac{0.2}{2} = 10\%$$

Whilst this does not stop the business from using more capital than is available, one can argue that since the return earned is greater than the cost of capital, the bank should simply increase its capital to take advantage of this excellent opportunity to earn excess returns. Indeed, if the cost of capital is set at the bank's actual cost of capital (or, even better, that of the individual business—this is something which is taken up in later chapters), then the calculation provides a simple benchmark: if the resulting return is greater than zero, do the trade; if not, don't do it.

There are some practicalities which have to observed here:

1. The definition of 'earnings' can be troublesome. If based purely on revenue, it will not necessarily result in positive returns for the bank, as the cost base also has to be covered. On the other hand, putting fully loaded costs into a pricing calculation will often result in trades with a positive marginal return being rejected (the fixed costs are not impacted by the addition of a single new transaction).

2. It may seem easy to argue that the bank should simply raise more capital if the returns which can be earned are greater than the cost of capital, but in practice this cannot be done so easily. On the other hand, there will not be that many opportunities in today's competitive markets which offer such superior returns—the issue may well be one of trying to find enough worthwhile transactions to utilise the existing capital base to its full capacity.

However, if applied sensibly, this model can be—and in the case of a few successful banks already is—the basis for a very solid risk-adjusted performance measure.

Treat the problem as one of solving dual constraints

Under this approach, the bank will try to maximise its return on economic capital whilst at the same time applying a constraint in terms of regulatory capital. This sounds like a simple linear programming problem for those readers who covered simultaneous equations in maths at school, but in practice it is not going to be so easy, especially if the bank wishes to use it as input for individual pricing decisions. However, as a broad level approach to allocating the overall capital to different businesses or divisions, it is simple, pragmatic and easy to understand.

Thus a business might be given a $1000 regulatory capital 'limit', within this limit, it will determine transactions based on the internal 'economic capital' model and performance measured on this basis.

Treat the capital requirement as the higher of regulatory and economic capital

This model is self-explanatory:

$$\frac{\text{earnings}}{\max \left[\text{regulatory capital; economic capital} \right]}$$

This is, however, a sub-optimal approach to capital allocation: it is almost inevitable that in some cases the regulatory capital will be higher, and in other cases the economic capital will dominate. If the full available capital of the bank is allocated to component businesses, the amount of regulatory capital utilised will be less than the total available regulatory capital, as will also be the case for economic capital, as illustrated in Table 3.7.

With $1000 of capital to allocate, the bank in this example only succeeds in making full use of $900.

Table 3.7   Optimising economic and regulatory capital

	Regulatory capital	Economic capital	Max (reg; econ)
Business 1	150	200	200
Business 2	150	200	200
Business 3	200	200	200
Business 4	200	150	200
Business 5	200	150	200
Total	900	900	1000

WHAT ABOUT THE LIABILITY SIDE?

It will hopefully not have escaped the notice of the reader that the regulatory capital approach looks only at the asset side of the balance sheet (including the contingent assets often classed as off-balance sheet instruments). Thus when allocating regulatory capital across businesses in any of the above models, this will be done according to the assets generated by those businesses. However, many banks may have businesses which seek to generate liabilities (such as deposits). Do these use regulatory capital?

Take as an example a bank which has matched customer assets and liabilities: for every $1 in customer loans it makes, it raises nearly $1 of deposits (it will not be quite $1, as the bank will have to put up capital for every loan). The loan and deposit functions are separate businesses, and the funds are transferred from one to the other at market rates. Without any regulatory or risk capital imputed to the liability side, the deposit business will appear to have infinite returns. But without a loan business in which to invest the funds, the bank would be forced to invest these in relatively risk-free assets such as government bonds or inter-bank deposits, which would bring lower overall returns to the bank.

One practical way of getting round this problem is to set an 'opportunity level' of regulatory or economic capital for the liability side. Thus it could be deemed that all deposits are invested in inter-bank loans, taking a 20% risk weight. An asset-generating business would then only be charged with the difference between the actual risk weight on its assets and the 20% floor. Whilst it could be argued that the appropriate transfer rate is that pertaining to government debt (0% risk weight), it should be borne in mind that investing liabilities priced off the short end of the yield curve in long-term bonds is certainly not a risk-free strategy, as the yield curve can easily invert.

In some situations, banks may be 'asset-driven'—that is to say, their capacity to generate assets exceeds their capacity to raise funds, and the difference has to be funded in the open market. In these cases, it may not be advisable to set a capital requirement on the liability side, or at least only at a very low rate, as management may wish to stimulate the raising of customer funds whilst ensuring that the asset-driven businesses are forced to meet tough hurdle rates. In other situations, banks may be 'liability-driven', implying that they have to invest surplus funds in the market. In these cases, management may wish to ensure that these businesses are picking up the full cost of the surplus assets which the bank is forced to generate.

SUMMARY

The international regulatory capital standards have developed considerably over the last 7 years, and we can observe a gradual convergence between the internal risk models used in banks and the tools required to calculate regulatory capital. However, it is to be expected that regulatory capital requirements will remain a relatively blunt instrument, appropriate for internal capital allocation only in those banks whose small size and homogeneous business mix do not justify the significant investment required to build an alternative, internal capital allocation model.

Regulatory capital remains a very important business constraint: not only is the amount of capital required a significant cost of doing business, but the penalties for failing to maintain legally required capital levels can also be severe. Various methods exist for combining the regulatory and in-house capital models: the problem can be seen as one which requires satisfying dual constraints, or alternatively the regulatory capital can be modelled in as an opportunity cost. There is no single correct answer, and each institution faced with this problem must choose an approach which is consistent with its situation, taking into account the kinds of constraints facing the bank (which is more important: maintaining a certain level of regulatory capital, or managing the earnings volatility to satisfy the stock market?) as well as the difficulties in getting staff to understand and adopt the model.

ENDNOTES

1. The delta of an option is a measure of the sensitivity of the option price to a movement in the underlying instrument. A delta of 0.5 means that, for every $1 in price change of the underlying instrument, the option price will move by $0.50. Thus owning call options on 100 stocks with a delta of 0.5 is broadly equivalent to owning 50 stocks in terms of the sensitivity to market moves. However, deltas are only part of the story with options, and the reader is advised to consult any one of the large number of excellent textbooks on derivatives to gain a better understanding.
2. *Capital in Banking and Insurance: Current Practice and Future Impact*, Salomon Brothers, New York, April 1993.

4
Value-at-Risk and Capital Allocation: the RAPM Approach

Chapter 3 introduced the basics of the regulatory capital model, and defined this kind of model as an 'asset-volatility-based' approach. That is to say, in order to determine the amount of capital required, the potential volatility in the value of assets (broadly defined) is used to determine the potential loss to which the bank could be exposed. This chapter looks at the equivalent models which some banks have developed internally to provide a better allocation of capital. They are called 'equivalent' models because, in common with the regulatory model, an asset-volatility-based approach is taken.

WHAT IS RAPM?

Risk-adjusted performance measurement—or RAPM for short—has been one of the buzzwords of banking over the last five years or so. The term actually embraces a whole bundle of concepts—indeed, just about every institution (be it a bank or a firm of consultants) which has introduced or is toying with RAPM will give a different definition of what it means. However many different flavours and labels one may encounter, all RAPM techniques have one thing in common: they compare return against capital invested by adopting some form of risk-adjustment, based on internal assessments of how risky something (an asset, a transaction, a business etc.) may be.

In all cases, this riskiness is judged by a statistical analysis of the potential volatility of outcomes (for example, the potential change in value of a particular asset). This is usually based on a technique called 'value-at-risk' (VAR). The main distinction between the RAPM model and the regulatory model is in a more precise, differentiated use of statistics, as the latter uses fixed risk-weightings as generalisations for the statistically expected change in value.

However, it is incorrect to think that the two different models are fundamentally different in all cases, and in fact in certain cases the different approaches can become so close as to be indistinguishable.

The four most commonly cited RAPM models are RORAA, RAROA, RORAC, RAROC. These come in two pairs; the first pair are asset-based, and are a derivation of that well-known banking ratio: return on assets (ROA). The second pair use a broader definition: return on capital rather than on assets. In each of the two pairs, the difference is whether the risk adjustment takes place in the numerator or the denominator.

RORAA **Return on Risk-Adjusted Assets.** This takes the ROA ratio, but instead of ranking all assets equally as in the ROA, the assets are adjusted to factor in their relative riskiness. Thus a loan to a corporate is weighted with a higher factor than a loan to a G10 government. This is essentially the approach taken in the Basle Accord of 1988.

RAROA **Risk-Adjusted Return on Assets.** This also uses the ROA ratio as its base, but the risk adjustment is made by deducting a risk factor from return. Thus if there were a 1% chance of a default occurring on a loan to a corporate in any one year, then 1% of the amount of the loan would be deducted from the return generated.

RORAC **Return on Risk-Adjusted Capital.** This measure starts off with the usual RoC measure, and replaces the regulatory capital in the denominator with an internal measure of the capital at risk. This is broader than the RORAA measure, as capital can be expanded to cover non-asset-based risks, such as off balance sheet products, or the foreign exchange risk of a trading position.

RAROC **Risk-Adjusted Return on Capital.** This uses the same basis as the RORAC measure—the starting point is return on capital—but instead of adjusting the denominator, the numerator is adjusted.

This list is by no means exhaustive: the same concepts may easily be encountered with a different acronym, or different meanings may be applied to the acronyms given here. However, at the root all of these techniques are variations on a common theme: the calculation is based on the potential volatility of the present value of a particular transaction. If a broad definition of the word 'asset' is used to mean the current net present value of any future cash flows, then these approaches can all be classified as 'asset-volatility-based' approaches.

THE LINK BETWEEN VAR AND OTHER CAPITAL ALLOCATION MODELS

The idea behind VAR is essentially the same as that behind regulatory capital, or indeed behind the general definition of capital established in Chapter 1: whereas provisions can be established to meet expected or likely risks, capital exists to absorb unexpected losses. VAR differs from the regulatory model in that it makes more rigorous use of statistical techniques and is broader in its coverage. For example, detailed analyses are made of likely loan defaults, which are then supplemented with factors which adjust for the level of diversification in the portfolio etc. Rather than relying on broad risk-weights (e.g. 8% for all corporate loans), the factors will take into account the credit rating of the counterparty, the tenor of the transaction, the type of security held etc. Further analyses might look at the potential loss which could be incurred by the trading book, probably even on a daily basis, and these will again be aggregated across different trading books, taking the effects of diversification across different trading portfolios into account.

However, it can be argued that the regulatory capital framework established by the Basle Committee in 1988 *is* a form of VAR: it does after all take a 'risk-weighting' against different classes of assets, based on some broad assumptions as to the likelihood of a collapse in value (see Figure 4.1). As the regulatory framework was of necessity fashioned in the crucible of political compromise, and had to cover a wide range of sophistication in banks, it is inevitably rather crude in its approach. RAPM is nothing more than a more refined, internally imposed regulatory capital regime.

Given the need to maintain regulatory capital levels, it is probably unwise to switch entirely to a VAR approach until it has been tried and tested for many years—otherwise there is a risk that the bank may expand beyond the regulatory measure of its available capital without realising it until it is too late. As with most performance techniques, it is unwise to put one's faith entirely in a single one—even Bankers Trust, which probably has the most rigorously applied and long-standing RAPM of any bank, does not rely on its RAROC blindly, but supplements it with other measures when making business decisions.

Ironically, despite the similarity between the regulatory approach set out in the Basle Accord and a rudimentary RAPM system, it was the Basle Accord which actually provided the impetus for banks to develop their own RAPM systems. This is because the banks were forced by the Accord to increase their capital levels quite significantly—and at a time when the banks were producing returns on their existing capital base which in some cases barely even covered the opportunity cost of investing in virtually risk-free government bonds. In order to improve the yields on their capital, banks were obliged to find ways to improve the efficiency of their capital allocation. One can paraphrase the banks' reaction as saying: 'OK, so we have to hold all this capital, but we are not going internally to weight all corporate loans with 8%!'

With the notable exception of Bankers Trust—which set up its RAROC system long before the 1988 Basle Accord was promulgated—the drive to implement RAPM has become very much a feature of the post-Accord banking environment. It is interesting also to note that whereas US banks have relatively sophisticated capital allocation techniques, the Europeans are less far advanced and the RAPM concept is virtually unknown in France or Japan. One suspects that this reflects the competitiveness of the capital markets in the various countries: both Japan and France have very protective and restrictive banking sectors, and there has been less pressure on banks to improve their returns.

THE RORAC AND RAROC MODELS

These two models are becoming the most widespread, replacing the RORAA and RAROA models. This mirrors the way that RoC (and its sister ratio, ROE) have replaced ROA as a key banking ratio: the problem

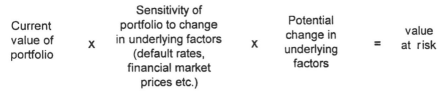

Figure 4.1   Essential components of asset-volatility approaches

with the asset-based measures is that they do not properly take into account the fact that much banking business is no longer on the balance sheet. Using capital gets round this problem, as capital can be defined as acting as a buffer against all unexpected losses, including those not incurred on the balance sheet (such as the potential loss arising from a foreign exchange position, or a derivatives trading book).

Both the RAROC and RORAC models start with the RoC formula (return divided by capital). More specifically, return nearly always includes operating costs, not just gross revenues, and may even go as far down as post-tax profits. Very often, the risk-free rate of return on the imputed capital is also added back. (As discussed in Chapter 2, it is possible to measure returns either on a 'gross' or a 'net' basis: under the former, the investment return includes the funding advantage of the capital invested, whereas the net basis excludes this funding advantage.)

Whilst RAROC adjusts the numerator (return) to take account of the various risks, the RORAC model adjusts the denominator (capital) to take account of the same risks. However, there is considerable confusion as to which is the right acronym for each approach, with some consultants using RORAC to describe something which other consultants would call RAROC.

A generic model, however you wish to call it, would be something like this:

$$RAPM = \frac{\text{revenues} - \text{costs} - \text{expected losses}}{\text{VAR}}$$

Expected losses typically cover statistically expected credit losses, which cannot be regarded as 'risk' (this argument is expanded later). The term VAR in the denominator is usually defined as 'capital necessary to cushion against unexpected credit losses, operating risks and market risks', and is often called 'risk capital' or 'economic capital'. After looking at the adjustment for expected credit losses, we will turn our attention to the various business-specific volatility drivers which make up the components of risk capital.

Many banks have taken the route of gradual implementation: rather than building the perfect RAPM model from scratch, they have started with a model which covered one major risk type (e.g. credit risk), and have slowly expanded and refined it over the years. Also, some banks may choose to take a fairly subjective approach to certain risks which are difficult to quantify: Chase Manhattan's model, for example, apparently adds on a factor for operational risk which is not mathematically derived, but which represents management's best guess as to the operational risk premium required in different businesses. There is nothing wrong with this approach—it is arguably better than relying on a purely statistical approach which may be fraught with hidden assumptions. Management does however need to be aware that by setting different risk premia against different activities, it is going to influence the behaviour of managers within the firm to prefer certain activities over others, and getting the balance wrong can have negative consequences.

ADJUSTING FOR EXPECTED LOSSES

This is a crucial adjustment which is often overlooked, as many people confuse the difference between expected defaults and the real risks in the credit business. Not adjusting for expected losses is like an insurance company taking in premiums and hoping that nobody ever makes a claim. The incidence of defaults is part of the business of credit, and the cost of those defaults is a routine cost of doing business. (As an aside, it has always annoyed the author that banks treat loan losses as something that happen way down the bottom of the profit-and-loss (P&L) account: they should really be deducted directly from revenue. After all, in the trading business, one also expects to lose money periodically, but nobody would suggest that trading profits be treated as revenue but trading losses taken down the bottom of the P&L, somewhere between depreciation and taxes!). Indeed, factoring in expected loan losses is something which every bank should do in its management accounts, even if it is not trying to build a risk capital model.

Chapter 7 will demonstrate in more detail the statistical loan loss model which has been adopted by many large banks. In summary, this requires structuring the credit exposures of the bank according to counterparty rating and tenor, and then multiplying this by the statistically expected default rate. For example, it might be expected that 0.1% of all credits with a tenor of 2 years and counterparties rated A will default some time between now and maturity. Therefore the total 2-year exposure to all counterparties rated A is multiplied by 0.1%. This is done for every combination of rating and tenor (this can be envisaged as a matrix with tenor on one axis and rating on the other) and the resulting total is the statistically expected loss for the credit portfolio as a whole. The change in this amount from one period to the next can be charged/credited to the

P&L account, with any actual defaults later occurring taken out of the statistical reserve.

TYPICAL BUSINESS-SPECIFIC VOLATILITY DRIVERS

Before examining the kind of risks which drive volatility in various business and suggesting how to measure them, the reader needs to be warned that what follows is no more than an introduction to the basic concepts: both credit risk and market risk deserve entire text books to themselves if they are to be covered properly. The generic points which are raised here should however be sufficient to put the technical issues covered in more specific text books in the proper context.

Different banking businesses have different levels of earnings volatility, due to the different risks which each incurs. Table 4.1 sets out the major volatility drivers which one might expect to find in each of those businesses, and notes whether they might be susceptible to statistical modelling. The table focuses on the main drivers and is not meant to be a complete catalogue of all possible risks.

The table shows that there are three main volatility drivers which can be represented, at least partly, by statistical techniques:

1. Market risk (exposure to changes in financial prices affecting the value of positions held by the bank, usually as part of its market-making or proprietary trading activities). This can come from foreign exchange rates, interest rates, equity markets, commodities etc.
2. Credit risk (exposure to loss of expected cash flows due to counterparty default)
3. Interest rate risk (exposure of the non-trading products of the bank to changes in interest rates).

Note that interest rate risk appears twice: once under market risk and once on its own right. This is because there are elements of interest rate risk which cannot be covered by the same approach as is adopted for the trading books.

DEFINING THE CREDIT RISK COMPONENT

There are essentially two factors which need to be modelled into the credit risk component: the volatility of the credit exposure itself, and the volatility of the default experience.

Volatility of exposure

With a traditional credit (a blank loan), the amount of credit exposure can clearly be determined in advance. If a bank lends $100 to someone, repayable on maturity and with no collateral, then the credit exposure is $100. (It might be argued that the exposure is slightly higher, as the bank hopes to earn interest on this loan, and at the same time has to pay refinancing costs—if the loan defaults, then the bank will receive neither principal nor interest, but will continue to have to finance the position. However, once a loan goes bad, a provision will be created by charging

Table 4.1

Business	Major volatility drivers	Statistical modelling?
Private banking/ asset management	• Exposure to change in financial markets (revenues are partly driven off portfolio value)	Yes
	• Exposure to financial market sentiment (greater portfolio activity in bull markets generates more fee income)	No
	• Credit risk exposure (loans to private clients)	Yes
Retail banking	• Credit risk exposure	Yes
	• Interest rate risk	Partly
Commercial banking	• Credit risk	Yes
	• Interest rate risk	Partly
Foreign exchange Trading & sales	• Market risk exposure (change in value of positions held)	Yes
	• Credit risk exposure (mainly derivatives)	Yes
Investment banking: Securities/ derivatives	• Market risk exposure (change in value of positions held)	Yes
Trading & sales	• Credit risk exposure (mainly derivatives)	Yes
Investment banking: Corporate finance	• Market risk exposure (primary positions etc.)	Yes
	• Credit risk exposure (e.g. loan products to corporate customers)	Yes
General (all businesses)	• Legal risk (risk that contracts might be annulled in court, or the bank sued for some perceived wrong)	No
	• Business risk (changes in the market, regulatory, competitive and other business environments)	No
	• Operational risk (risk that processing errors lead to losses)	No

an amount to the P&L account: this effectively means dipping into equity—as the net profit would otherwise be added to equity—with the result that the loan is now financed out of equity).

However, there are very few credit exposures which can be unequivocally quantified at the outset. Even straight loans can give rise to variable exposures, if they are collateralised by risky assets—the amount of the loan might remain unchanged, but the value of the collateral might change significantly, and the credit exposure should be properly defined as the difference. To account for this properly, the VAR model would have to allow for potential volatility in the price of the assets held as collateral. For financial assets, this could be approached using a similar methodology as outlined below for market risk, but bearing in mind that the period over which the asset is held is much longer than that used in the trading book.

For example, assume that the price of real estate in a given sector has fluctuated up and down over the years with a standard deviation of +/−10%. Management wants to use a higher level of confidence, and chooses to adopt 95% (1.96 standard deviations—see statistical appendix to this chapter). This means that they are 95% sure that the value of collateral will not fall by more than 19.6% in any one year.

Now imagine that a house owner is lent $90 000 to buy a house which is worth $100 000 (at least, that what he paid for it). He intends to repay the mortgage in instalments of $5000 per year over the next 18 years, and the bank holds the deeds to the house as collateral. What is the potential credit exposure?

The first thing to note is the 'square-root-of-time' rule (see Statistical Appendix (II) at the end of this Chapter)—the potential fall in house prices over two years at the 95% confidence interval is not twice 19.6%, but the square root of two times 19.6%, or 27.7% The expected amounts outstanding on the loan can be plotted against the potential value of the property (using the 95% confidence interval) to depict the credit exposure profile over the life of the mortgage. This is shown in discrete tabular form in Table 4.2, and graphically in Figure 4.2.

Note how the credit exposure first increases, as the potential negative change in house prices is greater than the reduction in the value of the loan. After a while, the loan repayments catch up with and then overtake the fall in the value of the collateral, and there is no net exposure. In this example, the maximum potential exposure over the lifetime of the mortgage is around $9200 (at the end of year 4). Although the numbers used here are only illustrative, this profile is not unusual for loans backed by

Table 4.2   Potential credit exposure on mortgage loan (95% confidence interval)

Time	Loan outstanding	Potential change in house prices (cumulative) (%)	Potential value of collateral	Potential credit exposure
0	90 000	0.00	100 000	0
1	85 000	19.60	80 400	4600
2	80 000	27.72	72 281	7719
3	75 000	33.95	66 052	8948
4	70 000	39.20	60 800	9200
5	65 000	43.83	56 173	8827
6	60 000	48.01	51 990	8010
7	55 000	51.86	48 143	6857
8	50 000	55.44	44 563	5437
9	45 000	58.80	41 200	3800
10	40 000	61.98	38 019	1981
11	35 000	65.01	34 994	6
12	30 000	67.90	32 104	0
13	25 000	70.67	29 331	0
14	20 000	73.34	26 664	0
15	15 000	75.91	24 090	0
16	10 000	78.40	21 600	0
17	5000	80.81	19 187	0
18	0	83.16	16 844	0

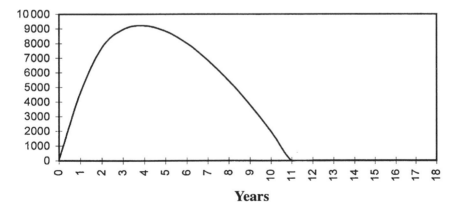

Figure 4.2   Potential credit exposure: mortgage loan (95% confidence level)

real estate as collateral. Note also that the number of $9200 is highly dependent on the confidence interval chosen. Using a higher confidence of, say, 97%, would result in a very different picture: in Table 4.3 and Figure 4.3 the calculations are repeated, but this time using 2.17 standard deviations (97%), or a potential annual fall in house prices of 21.7%.

Note that although the increase in standard deviations is only 10% (1.96 to 2.17), the maximum potential credit exposure is much higher, at around $13 500. The exposure also lingers on for longer than in the earlier example.

It is very important that this point is properly understood: given that this kind of analysis usually results in non-linear relationships (here because the loan amortises linearly but the collateral value in a logarithmic fashion), the difference between one confidence level and another is much more than a simple parallel upward shift in all of the numbers (which, since we are more interested in the relative returns of alternative business opportunities than the absolute amounts, would otherwise have

Table 4.3 Potential credit exposure on mortgage loan (97% confidence interval)

Time	Loan outstanding	Potential change in house prices (cumulative) (%)	Potential value of collateral	Potential credit exposure
0	90 000	0.00	100 000	0
1	85 000	21.70	78 300	6 700
2	80 000	30.69	69 312	10 688
3	75 000	37.59	62 414	12 586
4	70 000	43.40	56 600	13 400
5	65 000	48.52	51 477	13 523
6	60 000	53.15	46 846	13 154
7	55 000	57.41	42 587	12 413
8	50 000	61.38	38 623	11 377
9	45 000	65.10	34 900	10 100
10	40 000	68.62	31 379	8 621
11	35 000	71.97	28 029	6 971
12	30 000	75.17	24 829	5 171
13	25 000	78.24	21 760	3 240
14	20 000	81.19	18 806	1 194
15	15 000	84.04	15 956	0
16	10 000	86.80	13 200	0
17	5 000	89.47	10 529	0
18	0	92.07	7 935	0

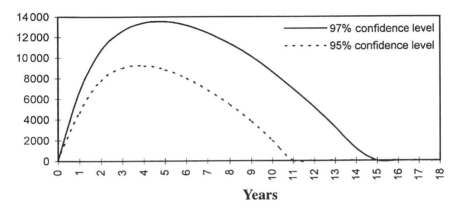

Figure 4.3   Potential credit exposure: mortgage loan (97% confidence level)

no effect on our decision). Using a 95% confidence interval in this example results in no net credit exposure from year 11 onwards, whereas
using 97% the exposure lingers on until year 14.

Similar analyses can be performed on almost any credit where the
amount of the exposure is dependent on the performance of some asset
over the lifetime of the transaction. In the above example, it was the value
of the collateral which depended on a statistical analysis—the value of the
loan itself was known precisely in advance. There are, however, several
credit products where the loan amount itself cannot be determined in
advance, and chief among these are derivatives and contingent credits.

Derivatives

Much has been written on the mathematical techniques required to model
the potential value of a derivative transaction over its life, and in particular the derivation of the potential volatility of the underlying financial
instrument can very quickly become too technical for anyone but the specialist. The mathematics are kept simple here, for the purposes of illustration—it is assumed that interest rates behave in a 'normal' fashion,
and that given the standard deviation of the annual change in rates the
'square-root-of-time' procedure can be used to forecast potential changes
over a longer period (in practice, a lot of refinements would be made to
make the model more precise, but these do not concern us here: the basic
point remains the same).

Table 4.4 shows a typical ten-year receive fixed/pay floating swap, with a notional amount of $100 million and annual coupon payments. At the time the swap is entered into interest rates are at 5%. The bank will receive $5 million every year, and will have to pay the equivalent floating rate. To avoid getting bogged down in complicated yield curve arithmetic, all future cash flows are discounted at 5%.

It is assumed that interest rates can move by 50 basis points per annum (one standard deviation), and using a confidence interval of 95% (1.96 standard deviations) gives a potential annual change in rates of 98 basis points.

Note that the final column—the present value of remaining payments—is always based on the value of the swap at that point in time. Thus in year three, it is assumed that there is a net receipt of $1.69 million each year for the remainder of the swap. Why not take the present value of the potential future payments ($1.96 million in year 4, $2.19 million in year 5, etc.)? This is because, in year 3, if the counterparty were to default the swap would automatically close out at current rates and the counterparty would owe the bank the present value of eight remaining annual instalments (including the one due immediately) of $1.69 each. Figure 4.4 reproduces the credit exposure profile in graphical form, showing maximum credit exposure peaking in year 4, at just under $12 million.

Table 4.4 Potential pay-off on fixed/floating swap (95% confidence level, all numbers in '000s)

Time	Receive fixed	Potential change in interest rates (cumulative) (%)	Potential pay floating	Potential net cash flow	Present value of remaining cash flows
0	5000	0.00	−5000	0	0
1	5000	0.98	−4020	980	7946
2	5000	1.39	−3614	1386	10 343
3	5000	1.70	−3303	1697	11 519
4	5000	1.96	−3040	1960	11 908
5	5000	2.19	−2809	2191	11 679
6	5000	2.40	−2600	2400	10 913
7	5000	2.59	−2407	2593	9654
8	5000	2.77	−2228	2772	7926
9	5000	2.94	−2060	2940	5740
10	5000	3.10	−1901	3099	3099
End	0	0.00	0	0	0

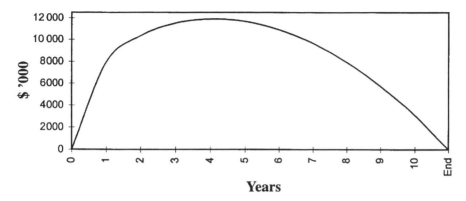

Figure 4.4   Potential credit exposure on interest rate swap (fixed/floating swap, 95% confidence interval)

It would be possible to create any number of such profiles, but the examples shown so far should be sufficient to illustrate the mechanics to the reader. The modelling of the potential credit exposure of options is similar to that for swaps, albeit with more complicated calculations.

Contingent credits

There are a number of credit products which exhibit an option-like character, in that they only convert into real credit exposure if they are 'exercised' by the holder. Typical examples are standby credit facilities, which the customer can draw down any time he wants. The procedure taken to model these is however exactly the same as that used for other credit exposures: one must first work out the likelihood of the credit crystallising, and then determine how big the exposure will be at that point in time. Whilst it may be theoretically possible to use an option-like valuation model, it is doubtful whether it is really feasible to derive a meaningful distribution of the probability of exercise, and it may be more pragmatic just to convert these to credit equivalents based on a historical average (e.g. assume that 50% of all standby credits are converted each year, i.e. 75% after two years, 87.5% after 3 years etc.).

Volatility of default experience

A further factor which determines the volatility of credit exposure is the potential change in default rates, which are partly linked to cyclical factors in the economy as a whole. In the example given earlier in this chapter, it was assumed that a loan with an A-rated counterparty and a two-year tenor had an expected default rate of 0.1%, giving rise to a loss of $1 per $1000 face over the two years. However, analysis of the history of default rates shows that these averages can change dramatically from year to year. Table 4.5 shows a comparison of the average default rates over 20 years as measured by Moody's[1] with the standard deviation of those rates over that period, as well as maximum and minimum values. The table only shows the information for 2-year exposures, but it can be constructed for each time bucket for which sufficient data is available. Note that the rating refers to the original rating at the time the bond was issued, and the default rates to the cumulative default rate over the lifetime of the bond. Thus on average 0.1% of all two-year bond issues rated A on issue defaulted at some time between issue and maturity.

These kinds of statistics are worth a study in themselves: one can derive all kinds of fascinating insights (such that the likelihood of a downgrading during the life of a bond is higher than that of an upgrading; also AA credits with very long maturities—over 15 years—actually have a lower cumulative default rate than AAA credits). However, one has to be very careful of the old adage 'there are lies, damned lies and statistics' with this sort of analysis, as the relatively short period involved and sometimes the limited number of issues in a particular class can distort the picture. For example, few issues are rated AAA, and it only takes one to go into default to increase the average AAA default rate significantly. For instance, Table 4.5 shows that the maximum experienced default rate in any given set of 2-year issues rated Baa was 1.3%. The average was 0.5%, and the standard deviation (derived purely arithmetically) was 0.4%, and taking a 99% confidence level (2.57 standard deviations [2] would suggest a potential default rate of 1.53% (2.57 times 0.4,

Table 4.5 Corporate bond default rates 1973–1994: 2-year cumulative rates

Rating	Average (%)	Standard deviation (%)	Maximum (%)	Miniumum (%)
AAA	0.0	0.0	0.0	0.0
AA	0.0	0.1	0.3	0.0
A	0.1	0.1	0.3	0.0
Baa	0.5	0.4	1.3	0.0
Ba	4.4	3.0	10.5	0.5
B	14.8	5.3	22.2	3.0

Source: Moody's Investors Service

plus 0.5)—higher than the highest-experienced rate! Given the non-normality and other limitations of the default statistics, it is probably much better to simply take the highest experienced rate and ignore confidence intervals.

Calculating the credit risk component

Thus in addition to having to calculate that our exposure might change over time (due to changing value of collateral etc.), we also have to reckon with the expected default rate increasing.

In the earlier example of the interest-rate swap the potential credit exposure, measured at a 95% confidence level, peaked at roughly $12 million. The average exposure over the life of the swap is around $9 million (found by averaging the values in the right-hand column of Table 4.4). Assume that the swap issuer was rated AA at the time the transaction was entered into. Assume also that the average cumulative default rate for an AA-rated borrower over 10 years is 1%, and that the maximum observed value for the same class was 2%.

The expected loss on this credit would normally be set as the average expected credit exposure multiplied by the average default rate (see Figure 4.5), giving $90 000. As described earlier, this expected loss would normally be treated as a cost of doing business, and charged to statistical credit loss reserve, held against future actual loan losses incurred.

In order to compute the value-at-risk, the maximum potential loss is computed first, and then the expected loss which was already accounted for is deducted (Figure 4.6).

Even on the basis of these simple examples, it becomes readily apparent that quite considerable computing power can be required to do these

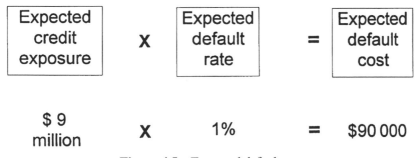

Figure 4.5   Expected default cost

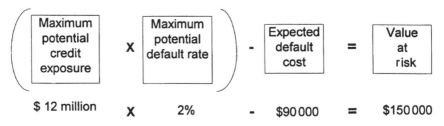

Figure 4.6   Value at risk: swap credit exposure

calculations, especially once portfolios with tens of thousands of open engagements in them are considered. This is one of the problems of the asset-volatility-based approach: the trade-off between precision and cost can be quite acute. Indeed, the fun with asset-volatility-based approaches is that one can never stop refining the statistics. For example, the use of the maximum potential credit loss multiplied by the maximum potential default assumes that the two 'peaks' occur simultaneously. A more sophisticated approach would be to compare the projected likely change in default rates over time with the projected potential credit exposure over the same period, and then take the combination of each which produces the highest value—this is not recommended, incidentally, as there are so many other assumptions already inherent (to what extent are future default and interest rates going to be consistent with the past? To what extent are the average default rates—here based on the entire universe of bonds rated by Moody's—consistent with our own credit portfolio?) That further refinements bring very little more than gratuitous fun to the statisticians who like doing this kind of thing: the improvement in 'accuracy' is very spurious.

DEFINING THE MARKET RISK COMPONENT

The approach to measuring market risk capital is in principle the same as that demonstrated for credit risk: take the value of the portfolio at a given point in time, calculate its sensitivity to potential changes in underlying factors, calculate the potential change in those underlying factors and multiply the sensitivity by the potential change (see Figure 4.1).

For example, the bank might be holding a long position in pounds sterling in the amount of £20 million, and the bank's base currency for currency trading is USD. Statistical analysis of past movements indicates that sterling can typically move by ±2% on any day against the dollar, measured as one standard deviation of the distribution of daily price changes; the bank wishes to use a higher confidence interval of 95%. Sterling is currently trading at 1.60.

The first thing to note is that a *holding period* and a *confidence interval* have to be specified. The holding period represents the period of time over which expected price movements are calculated (in this case one day), which implicitly suggests that the position can be liquidated within one day. (This might be a reasonable assumption for a small position in a highly liquid currency pair, but thus will not always be the case for larger positions or less liquid instruments.) The confidence interval then determines how many standard deviations of the price change distribution are to be used, with a higher number bringing a greater degree of confidence, as it represents a higher probability. For the sake of simplicity, two standard distributions are used (actually a 95.5% confidence level).

The calculation of the value at risk is shown in Figure 4.7.

Of course, one could have just used common sense and taken 4% of $32 million to arrive at a value at risk of $1.28 million, but this method of breaking positions down to their sensitivities to a particular factor and then multiplying the sensitivity by the potential change in factor makes it much easier to deal with large portfolios with many positions, and in particular where a particular product is exposed to more than one risk factor (for example a forward currency transaction, which is affected by both exchange rates as well as interest rates).

Another example, this time with two equity positions, will help illustrate how the decomposition/aggregation process might work: assume that the bank currently holds a long position of 1800 IBM shares at $90 per share, and a short position of 1000 GM shares at $50 per share (readers might like to refer back to the example given in Chapter 3, Table 3.6, to see the similarity between the value-at-risk approach to market risk

Current value of portfolio		Sensitivity of portfolio to change in underlying factors (default rates, financial market prices etc.)		Potential change in underlying factors		Value at risk
	X		X		=	
£20 million at 1.60 = $32 million	X	$0.016 per one percentage point in change in value of £1	X	4% move (2 std deviations)	=	$1.28 million

Figure 4.7   Value at risk on FX position

capital and the proposed regulatory approach). The standard deviation of the daily return on US stocks has been around 1.5% (this is just an example); the same holding period and confidence assumptions are used as in the previous example.

Before the example can be completed, however, one new piece of information is needed: the correlation between IBM and GM stocks. As the bank is long IBM, it is exposed to a fall in prices, whereas with the short position in GM it is exposed to rising prices. Clearly, it would be unwise to offset the two positions completely, as there is no guarantee that if IBM falls, GM will fall with it. On the other hand, the bank would be grossly overstating its risks if it took no account at all of the fact that, when the stock market falls, most stocks fall with it. This can be done by specifically calculating the distribution of returns on each of the two stocks, and calculating the historical correlation between the two. However easy this might seem when we are faced with only two stocks, the problem starts to become unmanageable when there are many stocks in the portfolio. The short cut developed to get round this problem is to use the beta of each stock as a measure of the stock's overall sensitivity to the market, and then use the overall potential change in the market as the sensitivity factor. Assume that the betas of IBM and GM are 1.2 and 0.8, respectively; the value at risk calculation is shown in Figure 4.8.

The net value at risk is $5832 minus $1200, or $4632. It is important to remember that the test is two-tailed: if the IBM stock position had been short and GM long, then the answer would still have been a potential loss of $4632.

Current value of portfolio	X	Sensitivity of portfolio to change in underlying factors (default rates, financial market prices etc.)	X	Potential change in underlying factors	=	Value at risk
IBM						
1800 shares at $90 = $162 000	X	1.2% per 1% change in market	X	3% move (2 std deviations)	=	$ 5832
GM						
-1000 shares at $50 = -$50,000	X	0.8% per 1% change in market	X	3% move (2 std deviations)	=	-$1200

Figure 4.8   Value at risk on equity position

This approach to calculating market risk capital is becoming the accepted standard in the banking industry, at least amongst those banks which are active as traders or market-makers of financial products. The best-known version of this approach is the *RiskMetrics* system developed by J.P. Morgan and released to the public in 1994. Contrary to some press comment, this system does not actually calculate the potential loss arising from a portfolio: what it does is provide the parameters (market moves given a certain holding period and confidence interval, and the correlations between the different sensitivity factors) which one needs to perform the calculations; a number of front-office software suppliers will however accept the parameters from the *RiskMetrics* system and perform the calculations. The RAROC system adopted by Bankers Trust also uses a VAR approach to measure market risk.

The usual system for calculating VAR is to break out the sensitivities into a number of broad risk classes (foreign exchange, interest rates, equities and sometimes also commodities), and then to establish risk factors within each. For foreign exchange, the risk factors will usually be currency pairs (often normalised against the US dollar: a position in DEM/STG can be seen as two positions, one in DEM/USD and the other in USD/STG). In interest rates, each currency has its own interest rate volatility, and within that a sophisticated system will differentiate between the volatility of short-term rates and that of long-term rates (for example, the proposals on regulatory capital requirements for market risk—see Chapter 3—require that the internal model be capable of breaking the yield curve into at least six different 'time buckets', each with its own sensitivity). In equities, the usual short-hand method, as seen above, is to convert all stocks into general market equivalents by multiplying the position by its beta, and then using one sensitivity for each equity market.

It would seem, then, that the only barriers to coming up with a rigid market risk capital system based on the VAR concept would be portfolio management or trading support systems which hold sufficient information in respect of current positions to enable the decomposition by risk factors, and the availability of statistical analyses to multiply and aggregate the sensitivity to risk factors. A host of software firms supply the former, and *RiskMetrics* supplies the latter. (One does not actually need *RiskMetrics*, incidentally—a decent database such as Datastream or Bloomberg, some statistical expertise and a reasonably powerful PC are all that are required to run the calculations oneself.) Unfortunately—or perhaps fortunately, in the eyes of the consultants who depend on this for a living!—things are not quite so simple, and there are four problem areas which require great care. These problems are all related to the nature of statistical analyses, and whilst they are addressed here in the context of measuring market risk, they are equally valid for the statistical measurement of credit risk.

Problems with holding periods

One problem arises out of the choice of the appropriate holding period to use. It was noted above that the assumption of a 24-hour liquidation period is probably reasonable for a small position in a liquid currency pair, but what about other markets and instruments? A large position in equities or a less-liquid currency pair is probably going to be harder to get rid of, as many banks found to their cost when the periodic boom markets in such instruments as perpetual floating-rate notes, Japanese equity warrants or, more recently, Latin American debt, suddenly dried up. The size of the position is also relevant: it would be much less easy to liquidate a £2 billion position than the £20 million position we saw in our above example.

There is no easy answer to the issue of holding periods, particularly since the 'typical' liquidation period which can be observed in normal markets can rapidly deteriorate in a crisis—and it is probably only in a crisis that we wish to liquidate the position in a hurry! Bankers Trust apparently requires a *one-year* holding period to be applied to all positions.

The difference between holding periods is not simply one of grossing up the potential moves in the risk factors: the reader will already be alert to the 'square-root-of-time' issue when changing the time period over which the calculations are made. Thus if a bank wishes to use a holding period of one week (five trading days) and only has the daily standard deviation, the assumed weekly standard deviation will be the *square root of five* times the daily number. However, it is emphasised here that this is the *assumed* weekly standard deviation: in practice, financial markets do not behave in a 'normal' way and it is unwise to make too many assumptions based on statistical theory: it would be much more prudent to go back to the price history database and re-calculate the weekly standard deviation by creating a series of weeks from each consecutive set of five trading days.

To avoid confusion, it is very important when discussing value-at-risk calculations to state both the holding period and the confidence interval assumed. Using a daily holding period of one day and a confidence level equivalent to two standard deviations will often be shortened to 'two daily sigmas' (sigma being the Greek letter used in statistics to denote the standard deviation). A holding period of two weeks and a confidence interval of one standard deviation will be shortened to 'one two-weekly sigma', etc.

Problems with curved price/payoff profiles

Even bigger problems occur with the fact that many financial instruments exhibit a non-linear price/payoff profile. This phenomenon is particularly acute in the case of options, and is generally referred to as 'curvature'. It should however be borne in mind that even straight bonds behave in a slightly non-linear fashion if observed over a big enough change in interest rates. The terms 'non-linear' or 'curvature' mean that the price of the instrument may not change in equal amounts to the change in whatever underlying risk factor is relevant. For example, spot positions in currencies and equities are linear: a 1% move in the underlying FX or stock price means a 1% change in the price of the currency or equity position, and a 10% move implies a 10% change in the value of the portfolio.

Instruments which exhibit curvature do not behave in this linear way: the price of an option will change by varying amounts for a given move in the underlying instrument, depending on how much the option is in or out of the money, and how close it is to expiry. (The sensitivity of the option price to a small change in the price of the underlying is known as its delta; the change in the delta due to the curvature is known as the gamma of the option, but this is deserving of another text book in itself.)

Figure 4.9 gives an extreme example of the effect of curvature: the portfolio profile shown is typical in the case where an institution is a big

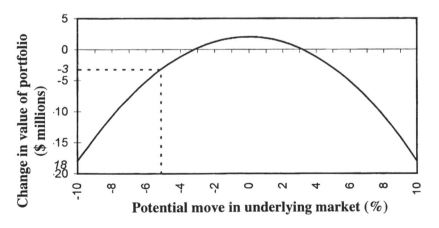

Figure 4.9 Value at risk: portfolio with curvature

seller of options (either because it is betting on markets trading a narrow range, or because its natural role is to create such products for the market, relying on constantly adjusting an offsetting position in the underlying instrument held as a hedge—'delta-hedging'—to provide some broad level of protection).

The x-axis of Figure 4.9 gives the potential move in the underlying risk factor (e.g. equity prices etc.), and the y-axis shows the resulting change in value of the portfolio. If the market remains in a narrow range, the position will show a profit, but once it moves in either direction by more than about 3%, the position starts to show a loss. At a 5% move, it shows a loss in value of $3 million, but at market move of 10%, the loss has increased to $18 million.

In other words, one cannot scale the potential loss calculated at a given holding period and confidence interval to another level, unless the extent of the curvature in the portfolio is known. Even if (and it is a big if) we know that a '2 daily sigma' move of 5% is actually equivalent to a '2 weekly sigma' move of 10%, we cannot take the VAR calculated at the 5% move and double it to arrive at the VAR at 10%, as the example in Figure 4.9 clearly showed.

Curvature can be shown up by increasing either the confidence interval or the holding period, or both, as both lead to greater potential moves in the underlying markets, making the choice of these parameters especially critical.

Problems with correlations

The penultimate set of problems encountered with VAR lie in the aggregation of the individual values-at-risk. The equities example above showed that the extent to which two different assets may be correlated with each other can be factored in, and this offsetting process continues to occur at each level of aggregation. Figure 4.10 illustrates this with a simple set of positions in two interest rates and two currency pairs. It can be seen that there are three levels of consolidation at which the correlation between two factors needs to be taken into account: firstly, across the yield curves within a single currency, then between the different yields and foreign exchange currency pairs, and lastly between interest rates and foreign exchange.

Whilst value-at-risk is a very good tool for monitoring the riskiness of a single risk factor, and perhaps even for allocating capital within, say, the interest rate trading area, the high reliance on correlations as one

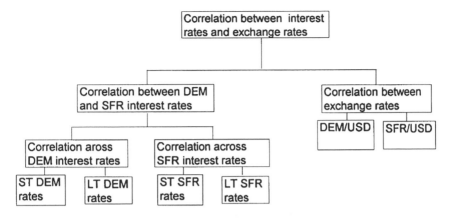

Figure 4.10   Example of correlation 'tree' in aggregating value-at-risk

moves up the aggregation 'tree' renders the numbers less and less reliable. This is because a correlation is a kind of average: it tells us, over a period of time (usually at least one years' worth of daily price movements are used, but some banks use five years or more), how the two variables behave in relation to each other on average over this period. There is no guarantee that they will behave in this way on any one day, and usually the point in time when the trader is relying most heavily on correlations to minimise his risk is the one point in time when the correlations break down: during a market crisis. Some correlations are so weak that they are deemed 'statistically insignificant' (significance tests are a statistical tool to see whether the results are really meaningful. Any pair of variables can be crunched to calculate a correlation, but the real issue is then how often the daily price moves actually conformed to this correlation, or at least close to it). Even worse, some correlations of pairs of risk factors even change sign (from positive to negative or vice versa) from time to time.[3]

Table 4.6 takes the example tree shown in Figure 4.10 and puts some numbers against the different sensitivities as examples. The method adopted to work out the consolidated value-at-risk at each node in the tree is explained in the statistical appendix to this chapter. It can be seen that the absolute value of all of the individual VARs is $75 000—this number assumes that the markets move in the unfavourable direction in each case. The first level consolidation allows for the fact that we are long in one instrument and short in another in each of three cases, adjusting for the level of correlation between each (thus the long and short positions in DEM rates cannot be totally offset to produce a net $5000 VAR, but actually have a combined VAR of $7483). The second level of consolidation allows some offset of the two different interest rates (DEM and SFR), and the final level of offset allows for the correlation between exchange rates and interest rates. The calculation of the combined VARs is not intuitively obvious, and is explained in the statistical appendix to this chapter.

Note that at each level, the absolute value of the VAR numbers is taken—the difference in sign and the level of correlation have not yet been taken into account, as this happens at the next level of consolidation. Thus before any consolidation we take each VAR number individually and ignore the sign (after all, the chance that the market goes down is the same as the chance that the market goes up).

The original VAR number of $75 000 very quickly reduces to just under $30 000, simply by taking the partial hedges within each risk factor into account. The next level of consolidation goes across risk factors (e.g. different interest rates) within the same risk class (all interest rate exposure is usually referred to as a 'risk class'), and brings the VAR down another $10 000 to below $20 000. The final level of consolidation —across risk classes—brings a further reduction of $4500, giving a final VAR number of only approximately $15 000.

This level of risk reduction is far from a technical detail: there is an enormous difference between comparing revenue with $75 000 of capital and with $15 000 of capital, and thus the correlation numbers become very important indeed. It has already been noted that correlations are not only unreliable, they can also change so significantly as to switch from positive to negative and vice versa. The higher up the consolidation tree we go, the more the correlations dominate the overall risk capital calculation: for example, eliminating the long position in DEM rates from Table 4.6 merely changes the overall VAR from $15 232 to $15 575—a change of only $343, or 2%. However, changing the correlation within SFR interest rates from 0.5 to 0.4 changes the overall VAR to $15 977—a difference of $745, or 5%. Higher up the tree, the effect becomes even more marked: changing all correlations by just 0.1 in the adverse direction takes the overall VAR up to nearly $20 000, equivalent to closing out the entire DEM/USD position (the spreadsheet used in Table 4.6 is easily constructed using the formula for 'normal' situations shown in the statistical

Table 4.6 Impact of correlations on aggegating value-at-risk

Risk factor	Example VAR	Correlation factor	First level consolidation	Correlation factor	Second level consolidation	Correlation factor	Third level consolidation
ST DEM rates	10 000						
LT DEM rates	–5000	0.69	7483				
ST SFR rates	–15 000			0.61			
LT SFR rates	10 000	0.50	–13 229		10 499		
DEM/USD	20 000		9220			0.19	15 232
SFR/USD	–15 000	0.90			9220		
Total	75 000		29 932		19 718		15 232

appendix: it is worth while building it and performing 'what-if' tests to see just how sensitive the total VAR can be to changes in parameters).

Problems with observation periods

Finally, management must also come to grips with the issue of observation periods. These determine the statistical parameters which are used both to calculate the sensitivity of individual risk factors and to determine the correlations used in the aggregation process.

When determining the potential change in price of a risk factor, one needs to observe the behaviour of that risk factor over a period of time, to work out the standard deviation of the price changes. The same process is needed to calculate the correlation between two risk factors, whereby the relative behaviour of the pair of factors over a period of time is observed. The observation period chosen to do this can be quite short (less than one year's worth of daily movements, for example), in which case the statistical distribution might not contain some of the more extreme events which can significantly increase the standard deviation. It will, however, give full weighting to more recent events, on the assumption that these have more bearing on the immediate future. The observation period might, however, be quite long—perhaps five years or more—in which case there is a greater chance that the occasional, more extreme events (such as the Crash of '87) have been captured, but also that events in the not-too-recent past (again, such as the Crash of '87) have been allowed to distort the picture. Sophisticated analyses like that used by J.P. Morgan's *RiskMetrics* do both, by using a long time period but then emphasising more recent experiences by applying a progressively higher weighting to these in the overall time series. However, at the end of the day it is a philosophical issue which only management can decide: no amount of high-powered mathematics can produce the single correct answer.

Alternative approaches to determining the market risk component

As a result of the above problems, a range of other techniques for determining the market risk component have been developed in recent years. Many of these techniques were actually developed to manage market risk limits better—their application to determining market risk capital was, at least in some cases, incidental. These alternatives to the 'variance/covariance' approach shown above include the following:

1. *Historical simulation.* Instead of relying on an assumed distribution which may or may not be normal, it is possible to rank the actual movements of a particular risk factor over a long period of time and then select the *n*th percentile. For instance, the daily movement in a pair of currencies might be mapped over 1000 trading days (roughly five years) and the 990th most severe move taken as the potential change in risk factor. The most severe moves are usually ignored for the purposes of value at risk, as they represent statistical 'outliers' with very low probabilities. This method can also be used to get round the problem of relying on unstable correlations: the worst possible combination of risk factors (or the *n*th percentile thereof) can be selected. However, as the combination of risk factors which produces the worst loss changes from day to day depending on the nature of the position being held, it is necessary to run the analysis every time risk capital is to be computed (usually daily in the trading business), which is not only time consuming but also costly in terms of computer power.
2. *Monte Carlo Simulation.* This technique again ignores historical correlations, and models the potential change in risk factor and the worst potential combination thereof (again, the *n*th percentile is more likely to be used). The technique is again very expensive in terms of both time and computer power.

DEFINING THE INTEREST RATE RISK COMPONENT

Whilst this might seem to have been covered by the market risk capital component, there are certain fundamental differences between the non-trading interest rate risk held by a bank and the interest rate risk in the trading book. These are due to:

- the longer holding period involved in the non-trading book (one cannot close out a loan as quickly as one can close out a bond position, and given the unique terms of some loans, it may also be difficult to find a perfect hedge);
- the fact that interest-rate sensitivity of the non-trading book is more difficult to model. A bond can be modelled relatively easily, as both the timing and the amount of the cash flows are known in advance (excluding default), whereas in the case of a mortgage portfolio or customer deposit accounts, it is much more difficult to determine either timing or amount in advance.

However, once a model to approximate the interest-rate sensitivity for these products has been built and empirically tested over time, the procedure for calculating VAR would be just the same as for credit risk or market risk: calculate the sensitivity of the portfolio to changes in the risk factors, model the potential change in the risk factors (given a certain level of confidence and a chosen holding period), and then multiply these out to work out the value-at-risk.

WILL RAPM SOLVE ALL MY PROBLEMS?

Whereas the asset-volatility approach will always appeal to the purists, it must be noted that very few banks have actually implemented such a model. Some banks have opted for part-implementation, for example in the investment banking arm, without trying to encompass the whole organisation. Only Bankers Trust appears to have made such an approach an integral part of their culture (the BT approach is very similar to the generic approach to credit and market risk illustrated above). Many banks have stuck to the regulatory model, and have still been successful—Lloyds bank is a classic example. The focus on a more traditional RoC was accompanied at these banks by good risk management and sound lending practices, and this probably lies at the heart of the issue: there is a risk with a highly statistical approach like VAR that it slips beyond the grasp of many in senior management, who then blindly trust the numbers without fully understanding their limitations.

The limitations of asset-volatility-based approaches are:

1. The high reliance on correlations can easily lead to big differences in the amount of risk measured. When the Basle Committee, in preparation for accepting the use of internal value-at-risk models for the purposes of calculating market risk capital (see Chapter 3), asked several leading banks to calculate the VAR on a number of test portfolios, the answers they received varied widely. Even once the Committee had stipulated both the confidence interval and the holding period to be used, the different observation periods used to ascertain both the individual risk factors and their correlations still resulted in significantly different total VAR numbers.
2. Whereas one can make a case for calculating a single value-at-risk number for all market risks, going to even higher levels of aggregation (e.g. adding market and credit risk together) is more problematic. Default rates are usually established on a yearly basis, and the desired holding period for the purposes of establishing risk capital is usually the full remaining period until maturity of the credit. How does this compare with the perhaps daily VAR in trading? (Bankers Trust partly gets round this problem by putting everything on an annual basis, but it could be argued that this is unduly conservative for the trading book and unduly optimistic for the loan book.)
3. The intense ex-ante modelling approach assumes that all risk factors can be identified and modelled. In the trading area, for instance, the assumption is that all volatility is due to the sensitivity of open positions. But even trading books which hold minimal positions—such as a pure market-maker—can suffer from significant revenue volatility as a result of such factors as market volumes and liquidity. A counter-argument in favour of the asset-volatility approach is that it provides a tool for measuring—and thus steering—those risks which management can control. If one cannot control the other risks, they are simply a cost of being in a particular business.

4. In the search for greater precision lurks the danger of overkill. For example, when looking at modelling the credit exposure on a mortgage, the potential change in value of the collateral based on an index of real estate prices was used—this could be segregated by type (commercial versus residential), and/or by region. Even within regions the volatility of prices may vary significantly, but at some point subdivisions are reached which are both prohibitively expensive to monitor and statistically unusable (as the sample size is too small to be representative of any meaningful population). The cost of computing power and mathematically gifted analysts can easily start to become very expensive. In addition, the finer and finer levels of granularity which the maths expert will by nature want to build into the models bring only a very spurious level of accuracy, given the other broad assumptions as to the reliability of correlations etc. which go into the model.

STATISTICAL APPENDIX (I): PROBABILITY DISTRIBUTIONS AND CONFIDENCE INTERVALS

A probability distribution is a statistical model of how often something occurs or is likely to occur. The most commonly encountered is the normal distribution, but there are others. In such a distribution, a measure called the standard deviation allows us to determine the probability of a particular event.

The area under the bell curve is equal to the total probability (100%). In a normal, non-skewed distribution, the curve is symmetrical, i.e. the probability on the left-hand side of the mean (or middle) is equal to the probability on the right. The standard deviation measures distances either side of the mean (see Figure 4.11).

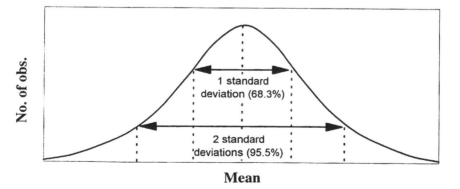

Figure 4.11   Normal distribution

For example, one standard deviation either side of the mean covers an area under the curve which is equal to 68.3% of the probability, whereas two standard deviations are equal to 95.5%. In technical terms, the standard deviation is derived by taking the square root of the variance, which is a measure of the spread of the variables either side of the average (mean). The variance—and hence also the standard deviation—is very easy to calculate from a series of variables (most pocket calculators and all PC spreadsheet applications can handle this with ease), and the relative probabilities for a given number of standard deviations can either be read off a printed table or produced by a formula in spreadsheet programs, making this a very simple but powerful tool.

Table 4.7 shows some typical probabilities and the related number of standard deviations under the normal distribution. A two-tailed test is used here (the probability is given by a symmetrical spread either side of the mean)—other tests are introduced in later chapters.

Table 4.7   Confidence intervals

Probability (%)	Number of std deviations
68.3	1.00
90.0	1.65
95.0	1.96
97.0	2.17
99.0	2.57

STATISTICAL APPENDIX (II): THE 'SQUARE-ROOT-OF-TIME' RULE

This rule often baffles people, as it is not intuitively obvious. As a result, it is often quoted as if it were some fundamental law of nature, whereas in fact its origins lie in a very simple aspect of the calculation of basic statistical data.

When we scale averages over a time period, we all know that we can simply multiply or divide by the relationship between the number of time periods. For example, if on average 100 people visit a particular cinema on any one evening, then we know that on average 700 people will visit the cinema over a week (assuming the cinema is open 7 days a week). Statistically, we can say that the mean of a sum of distributions is the same as the sum of the means.

The same is true of the variance of these distributions. If we know that the variance in the above daily cinema attendance figure is 10, then the weekly variance is 70—we can just add the numbers together. The variance is found by taking the difference between the individual observations and the average, and squaring this. We then add all the squares together, and divide by the number of observations to obtain the variance (actually, we divide by the number of observations if we are dealing with the full population—in this case, every evening on which the cinema has ever been open—and by one less than the number of observations if we are dealing with a sample. This is a statistical rule which just has to be accepted, as its derivation is beyond the scope of this book). Mathematically, this is expressed as:

$$\text{Variance} = \frac{\sum_{i=1}^{n}\left(X_i - \overline{X}\right)^2}{n-1}$$

We then recall that the standard deviation is obtained by taking the *square root* of the variance. Thus when scaling variances over time periods, we can simply multiply or divide, as is the case for averages, but the scaling of standard deviations needs to take into account the fact that square roots are involved. Therefore, when converting a monthly variance into an annual one, we multiply by 12, and the standard deviation of the annual distribution can be expressed as:

$$SD_{(\text{annual})} = \sqrt{\text{Variance}_{(\text{monthly})}.12}$$

$$= \sqrt{\text{Variance}_{(\text{monthly})}} \cdot \sqrt{12}$$

$$= SD_{(\text{monthly})} \cdot \sqrt{12}$$

As a short cut, the monthly standard deviation is simply multiplied by the square root of time. In our cinema example, the standard deviation of the daily attendance is the square root of 10, or 3.16228; the standard deviation of the weekly attendance is:

$$3.16228.\sqrt{7} = 8.37 \text{ which is equivalent to } \sqrt{70}$$

This procedure is valid only if we assume that the individual months are independent of each other; if there is any correlation between the results of the individual months, then a more complicated procedure is required to calculate the standard deviation of the combined period.

STATISTICAL APPENDIX (III): CORRELATIONS

As was seen with normal distributions above, one has to be very careful when combining different statistical measures. The proof of the formulae shown below can be found in most statistics text books, and does not need to be repeated here, but some general knowledge of these formulae and their application is fundamental to a proper understanding of how value-at-risk, and other asset-volatility-based approaches, can be aggregated to produce a single risk-capital number. Rather than produce the formula and show how it collapses into a simpler formula in the extreme cases, the extreme cases are taken first, as these are intuitively easier to understand for the non-statistician, and are used to show how the full formula leads to a result which is intuitively correct.

Extreme case: perfect positive correlation

This is the easiest case to deal with, and refers to the situation where the two variables always march in total unison. When two variables are perfectly positively correlated, the standard deviation of the combined pair of variables is equal to the sum of the standard deviation of the individual variables. This is expressed mathematically as:

$$\sigma_{(a+b)} = \sigma_{(a)} + \sigma_{(b)}$$

When the two variables are mixed in different quantities (i.e. they are not the same size), then this equation needs to be weighted with the relative proportions of a and b:

$$\sigma_{(a+b)} = \frac{a}{a+b}\sigma_{(a)} + \frac{b}{a+b}\sigma_{(b)}$$

The same rule can be applied to sensitivities to risk factors. In the example given in Table 4.6, the first pair of variables are the DEM short-term and long-term interest rates. The value-at-risk to a given move in interest rates (say, all move up by 1%—we call this a 'parallel shift' in the yield curve) is +10 000 and −5000. Which one is positive and which negative is not important (rates could just as easily fall 1%, in which the VARs would be −10 000 and +5000)—it is only important that they have opposite signs. The weighting shown in the above equation has already been done, as the sensitivities are expressed as dollar amounts (i.e. a percentage change based on a certain confidence interval multiplied by the size of the position). The sensitivities are calculated based on the same level of confidence (i.e. number of standard deviations), and therefore if the two interest rates are perfectly correlated, then if one goes up the other will go up, and we can simply add the two VARs to provide a combined VAR:

$$\text{Combined VAR} = \text{Sum of individual VARs}$$
$$10\ 000 - 5000 = 5000$$

This is intuitively obvious: if the two interest rates always move in parallel, then a move up in one must mean a move up in the other, and the gain on one position can be fully offset against the loss on the other. Note that in 'summing' the two VARs, the difference in sign is taken into account, but that subsequently only the *absolute value* of the result is relevant, i.e. sensitivities calculated against a fall in rates would still lead to a value-at-risk of $5000.

Extreme case: perfect negative correlation

This represents the opposite case to the extreme of perfect positive correlation. In this case, whenever one rate moves up, the other moves down. Common sense dictates that being long one rate and short the other could bring either a profit on both or a loss on both—as we are interested in risk, we do not know whether rates will go up or down, only that they can move, so we take the absolute value of the two potential moves and add them together.

More formally, the equation for two perfectly negatively correlated variables is:

$$\sigma_{(a+b)} = \sigma_{(a)} - \sigma_{(b)}$$

Again, the issue of weighting the relative standard deviations can be skipped as this is done for us in the calculation of the individual VARs:

$$\text{Combined VAR} = \text{VAR}_A - \text{VAR}_B$$
$$10\ 000 + 5000 = 15\ 000$$

Again, this is intuitively obvious: if we can lose \$10 000 when long-term rates go up, then we will also lose \$5000 on the short-term rates position as short-term rates go down.

Extreme case: zero correlation

In this case, the two variables are completely independent of each other: when one goes up, the other may go up, down or nowhere at all. The rule which applies in this case is that the standard deviation of the combined pair will be equal to the square root of the sum of the squares of the individual standard deviations (since the standard deviation is itself the square root of the variance, this can be more simply expressed as the 'the variance of the combined distribution is equal to the sum of the variances of the individual distributions'):

$$\sigma^2_{(a+b)} = \sigma^2_{(a)} + \sigma^2_{(b)}$$
$$\text{and thus } \sigma_{(a+b)} = \sqrt{\sigma^2_{(a)} + \sigma^2_{(b)}}$$

Since the VAR numbers are based on a standard-deviation move (or a multiple thereof), the VAR of the combined position can be calculated as the square root of the sum of the two VARs squared; again, the weighting of the two variables in the combined position is taken care of in the fact that the two VARs already have a relative size in \$-terms:

$$\sqrt{10\ 000^2 + 5000^2} = 11\ 180$$

This also makes intuitive sense: the zero-correlation scenario should lie somewhere between the perfectly positive and perfectly negative scenarios (but note that it is not exactly in the middle, as the weightings of the two positions are not equal).

Normal case: correlation is not +1, −1 or 0

We know from the example given in Table 4.6 that the correlation between short-term and long-term DEM interest rates is +0.69 (i.e. somewhere between 0 and +1), so we would expect the combined value-at-risk to fall somewhere between the \$11 180 calculated at zero correlation and the \$5000 calculated at a correlation of +1.

The full formula for calculating the variance of a pair of variables is as follows:

$$\sigma^2_{(a+b)} = \left(\frac{a}{a+b}\right)^2 \sigma^2_{(a)} + \left(\frac{b}{a+b}\right)^2 \sigma^2_{(b)} + 2\left(\frac{a}{a+b}\right)\left(\frac{b}{a+b}\right)\text{Cov}_{(a,b)}$$

Again, the weighting element can be eliminated, as the relative size of the VARs does this for us. The last expression in the equation uses the covariance, which can also be written as:

$$\text{Cov}_{(a,b)} = \sigma_{(a)} . \sigma_{(b)} . \text{Corr}_{(a,b)}$$

and therefore

$$\sigma^2_{(a+b)} = \sigma^2_a + \sigma^2_b + 2(\sigma_a . \sigma_b . \text{Corr}_{(a,b)})$$

Finally, we have to remember that in VAR we are dealing with numbers based on standard deviations, so we need to take the square root of the variance formula, giving us the following formula for the combined value-at-risk:

$$\text{VAR}_{(a+b)} = \sqrt{\text{VAR}^2_{(a)} + \text{VAR}^2_{(b)} + 2 . \text{VAR}_{(a)} . \text{VAR}_{(b)} . \text{Corr}_{(a,b)}}$$

However, we have to be very careful with the signs here, since the positions have opposite values. Since squaring a negative number gives a positive one, only the last of three expressions inside the square root actually comes out negative:

$$\sqrt{10\ 000^2 + (5000)^2 + 2(10\ 000 \times -5000)0.69}$$

$$= \sqrt{10\ 000^2 + 5000^2 - 2(10\ 000 \times 5000)0.69} = \$7483$$

ENDNOTES

1. See *Corporate Bond Defaults and Default Rates 1970–1994*, Moody's Investors Service, New York, January 1995, especially Tables 8 and 9 in the Appendix.
2. Throughout this chapter, two-tailed tests are used so as to avoid confusing the reader with different standard distributions for the same level of confidence. One-tailed tests are introduced in a later chapter.
3. I am grateful to Tom Wilson at McKinsey & Co. in London for this analysis and for the correlation factors used in the example in Table 4.6.

5

A Top-down Approach: Determining the Cost of Capital and The 'Earnings at Risk' Buffer

Chapter 1 looked at the different forces driving the level of capital which a bank may require: in addition to the regulatory minimum, there may be pressure from credit rating agencies and from the market (such as from depositors, if the competition is also highly capitalised) to maintain as high a level of capital as is possible. Against this must be set the pressure from the shareholders to achieve an optimum return on the capital which they have invested in the bank. It was noted that there is no magic formula which enables management to arrive at the optimum level of capital, but that management needs to weigh up three constraints in setting the appropriate level of capital:

- the minimum regulatory requirements for the planned level of activity, together with a small margin for error;
- the requirements of the credit rating agencies;
- the internal assessment of the riskiness of the activities to be undertaken.

Against these must be set the desire to keep capital as low as possible for a given level of return, so as to maximise the Return on Capital (RoC). This chapter introduces a basic model which enables us to make some judgements about the appropriate level of capital for different banks, and which can therefore be used to calibrate the economic or risk capital models developed in-house. Unlike the asset-volatility approach examined in the previous chapter, which relied on a bottom-up estimate of the value at risk of individual components and then aggregating these, the model used in this chapter uses a holistic, top-down view of the bank.

WHAT IS A SUITABLE TARGET RoC?

The question of capital levels can be phrased either way: given a certain amount of capital, how much return should we aim for? Or given a certain amount of planned return, how much capital should we hold? The key to both questions is the required RoC.

If the return required by shareholders is known, then it is possible at least to make a reasonable calculation: one can either start with a planned return (based on what can be achieved in terms of market share increases etc., i.e. an incremental approach), or one can start with a given level of capital and work out what sort of return needs to be generated (i.e. a zero-based approach).

One approach is to look at the returns generated by similar banks (benchmarking), and set a goal of simply beating the competition. This may be a good starting point, but if the average performance across the industry is poor, then this is probably not very ambitious, and may over time expose the bank to the risk of a take-over. Whilst most bank take-overs and mergers have been either smaller, troubled banks being acquired by their larger brethren, or the merger of two similar size banks, there is no reason to believe that the large banks are any longer safe from predators. Even stable Switzerland has seen in the last year an attempt by an aggressive investor (Martin Ebner's BK Vision) to acquire a controlling stake in UBS and force change of strategy, with the express purpose of improving the return to shareholders. The threat of take-over is anyway a rather negative motive for management—they are employed to obtain the best possible results for shareholders, not to defend their own jobs!

USING CAPM TO ASSESS COST OF CAPITAL

It is one of the fundamental tenets of modern portfolio theory (the underpinning of all modern financial mathematics) that there is a relationship between the expected or required return on a particular asset and the uncertainty surrounding that return. This uncertainty is expressed in the form of the standard deviation of the return.

This approach is best known in the form of the Capital Asset Pricing Model (CAPM).[1] A lot has been written on the CAPM, which is a core part of any corporate finance curriculum. (Recently, some commentators have called the CAPM into question, arguing that the statistical analysis which underpins it is not reliable. However, it is still an appropriate tool for management to use to make what is eventually a 'soft' decision—an estimate of the bank's cost of capital).

The model states that the required return on an investment (R_i) can be determined by reference to the historical relationship between the investment and the market:

$$R_i = R_f + \beta(R_m - R_f)$$

where R_f refers to the risk-free rate, and R_m to the market return. The expression in parentheses $(R_m - R_f)$ refers simply to the excess return of the market over the risk-free rate (the risk premium). The beta is a factor for each individual stock which measures how closely the stock follows the market. A stock with a beta of 1, for example, will have the same expected return as the market. Thus the expression $\beta(R_m - R_f)$ is the risk premium attaching to an individual stock. The risk premium is calculated as an add-on to the risk-free rate, as the latter fluctuates over time but the long-term risk premium should remain fairly constant.

For example, if the market typically generates 5% more than the risk free rate, and the risk-free rate is 6%, then the expected return (and hence the cost of equity) for an institution with a beta of 1.2 will be:

$$6\% + (1.2 \times 5\%) = 12\%$$

A bank can approach this in two ways: it can use its own historical beta to calculate the cost of equity, or it can use the beta of its benchmark competitors. Its aim must be to improve on its own rate of return: simply earning the cost of equity will maintain shareholder value, but not increase it.[2] The benchmark return could be a good target, or a more ambitious bank could even aim to beat this benchmark. The typical betas of a variety of different banks are given in Table 5.1.

Note that, when using CAPM to set a benchmark, the risk-free rate is based on a forecast over the planning horizon, not the current rate, as the model is being used to calculate the future cost of capital. Both the market premium and the beta can be strongly influenced by short-term trends in the stock market (it is perfectly possible for the market return to be negative, even over a number of years) and therefore a very long-term estimate of the equity market premium is used—20 years is very often adopted as the minimum. The equity risk premium is typically around 5%, and this is a good rule-of-thumb number for the US and UK, with a slightly lower premium of around 4% typical for continental Europe.

Table 5.1 Typical betas for different types of bank

	Median	High	Low
Universal banks	0.97	1.28	0.86
Trading and investment banks	1.16	1.41	1.07
Global investment banks	1.51	1.61	1.14
Asset mgt—private	1.31	2.03	0.81
Asset mgt—institutional	1.21	1.66	0.97
Retail banks	1.09	1.52	0.74
Overall	1.11	1.51	0.87

Betas should also be calculated over long periods, although it is not necessary to do the calculations oneself: market data services such as
Datastream provide perfectly good betas, as do many of the stock market
analysis departments of leading investment banks and stockbrokers.

Having calculated the percentage return to which the bank aspires,
management can compare this against the return on capital for the bank
as a whole implied by the business plans, as well as with past performance. If the answer is below the target, then management must consider
either improving the net profit or reducing the capital, or both. Due to the
long-term nature of capital, changing the denominator in the equation
(capital) is more difficult than influencing the numerator (return i.e.
profit)—it is difficult to change capital levels over the short term,
although raising more capital is usually easier than reducing an existing
capital surplus.

The target RoC implied by the market is also a good internal discount
factor to use when assessing the viability of additional projects (this is the
classic use of CAPM-derived discount factors throughout all branches of
the private sector). Thus the cost of capital of the bank is equated with the
minimum return on capital which the bank must strive to attain. This is
always a very good starting point when assessing appropriate capital levels: any bank activity which cannot earn at least its cost of capital is not a
viable activity. This is clearly easy to measure at the level of the bank as a
whole, but becomes critical when looking at individual activities of businesses within the bank. The key question then is how to allocate capital
fairly across businesses, as an incorrect capital allocation will lead to an
incorrect calculation of the return on capital, which will in turn lead to
incorrect decisions as to which businesses are most viable.

There are, however, limitations to using market-expected returns to set RoC targets—Chapter 8 looks at some of these in more detail. Despite these limitations, it is clearly important for banks to try and improve the return on the capital invested, and allocating the available capital efficiently is central to achieving this improvement: a rough guide to required returns is better than no guide at all.

THE RISK/RETURN RELATIONSHIP AS A DETERMINATE OF REQUIRED RETURNS

The stock-specific factor in the CAPM is the beta. This is calculated as the covariance of the returns of the stock and the market, divided by the variance of the market return. Beta can however be written differently, in a way which is much more intuitive to the non-statistician.[3]

$$\beta = \text{Corr}_{i,m} \frac{\sigma_i}{\sigma_m}$$

Beta consists of two components: the correlation between the investment (i) and the market (m), multiplied by the level of volatility of the investment relative to the market (the term σs is statistical shorthand for the standard deviation). The correlation term tells us how closely the stock follows the market's *direction*: most stocks are quite strongly correlated to the market, but different sectors of the economy may have different correlations. The second component of the formula relates the standard deviation of the return on the stock with that of the market: it gives an idea of the *size* of the movement on the stock return.

Given equal correlation, the betas of different stocks will be determined only by the volatility of the returns on those stocks. Making a small leap of faith, it can be assumed that all banks are highly correlated with each other (it does not require a financial analyst to observe that banks really do seem to behave as a herd, reporting good years and bad years together), and that therefore the different betas observed in the market must be due only to the different levels of volatility. Making another small leap of faith, one can hypothesise that the volatility of the stock price is influenced almost entirely by the volatility of the earnings of the bank in question.

Modern portfolio theory teaches that there is a trade-off between the required return and the riskiness of that return (i.e. the volatility). This is clearly seen in the betas shown above: the higher earnings volatility in the trading activities in which the investment banks engage is reflected in much higher betas for those institutions—in other words, the stock market investor requires a higher return on average to compensate him for the fact that the return each year may be very different from that average.

It can therefore be postulated that there must be a relationship between the returns required by the market and the volatility of banks' earnings. Bank managements often set themselves targets for RoC without considering this relationship. It is not enough to set a target of 15% RoC without considering a target for volatility as well. One bank may be able to produce a steady 10% RoC without any fluctuation, whilst a bank which has more volatility in its earnings may need to produce a much higher average return to compensate shareholders for the uncertainty.

Imagine two banks: Bank A and Bank B. Each has capital of $10 billion and average earnings of $1 billion (a 10% return on capital). However, in the case of Bank A, the earnings tend to fluctuate quite wildly: some years $500 million, and then $1500 million in the next year. Bank B, on the other hand, earns very close to the average every year.

The deliberations on financial market theory above suggest that the market value of Bank A's stock will be below that of Bank B (assuming that the expected growth rate of future average earnings is the same in both cases), as investors will require a higher return on Bank A's stock to compensate them for the higher volatility. Bank A's management must therefore set itself the target of improving the RoC above that of Bank B, in order to bring the market value of the bank back up to Bank B's level.

And indeed, looking at the betas of quoted banks and the volatility of their returns, one can see that there is a very close relationship between the two. Figure 5.1 plots the betas of a range of leading international banks against their revenue volatility (revenues are used instead of earnings, partly because much of the volatility in earnings comes from revenues, but also because this links better into the earnings-volatility-based capital allocation model which we will encounter in the next chapter). The revenues have been normalised over time by reference to changing capital levels, to make the series based on a constant mean. The volatility of revenues is expressed as one standard deviation divided by the mean. One can see that there is in fact a very good relationship between revenue volatility and betas: the 'r^2' measure is a statistical measure of how well the observed data fit the regression line drawn in, and a value of 0.85 is indeed very high.

The regression analysis was performed on some 25 banks from different countries, with two extreme 'outliers' later removed to avoid distorting the

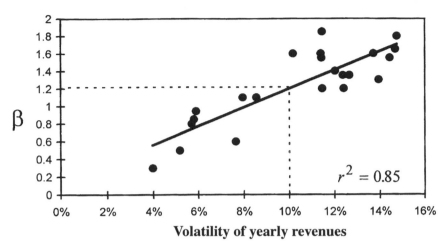

Figure 5.1 Regression of beta against revenue volatility

picture, over a period of 10 years. The revenues over this period were normalised by adjusting for the growth trend over the period, as $100 in revenue in 1984 is not necessarily comparable with $100 ten years later (this adjustment is explained in more detail in the section on standard errors in the statistical appendix to Chapter 6).

Thus given a market risk premium of 5% and a risk-free rate of currently 6%, one can derive an estimated cost of capital for a bank with revenue volatility of 10%—reading off the graph, this gives a beta of 1.2, and thus a cost of capital of:

$$6\% + (1.2 \times 5\%) = 12\%$$

Table 5.2 translates the regression into a table from which the appropriate beta can be read.

This is an extremely useful analysis, as it moves beyond the historical beta and resulting CAPM-driven cost of capital, to a model which allows management to assess business plans based on their riskiness. Whilst in the case of a bank which is quoted on the market one can simply use the historical beta, this model enables CAPM to be applied in three circumstances where historic betas cannot be observed:

1. When performing 'what if' calculations in respect of future plans. These might result in a very different risk/return profile than the bank has traditionally had, which could result in a change in the stock market's expected return. This model can be used to work out what that expected return is likely to be.

Table 5.2 Derivation of beta from revenue volatility

Std. dev. of annual revenues as % of average	Modelled Beta
4	0.58
6	0.79
8	1.00
10	1.22
12	1.44
14	1.65
16	1.87
18	2.09
20	2.30

Based on the regression, beta = 0.14 + (10.82 × volatility)
The numbers in the table have been rounded slightly

2. When the bank in question is not quoted, or has not been quoted long enough to derive an observed beta.
3. When calculating the cost of capital for component businesses within a bank.

A TOP-DOWN MODEL OF EARNINGS AT RISK

Assume that Bank A has a historical revenue volatility of 10%; the market premium is usually 4%. Using the table derived above, a 10% volatility indicates that the beta should be 1.22, which translates into a risk premium for the bank of roughly 5% (1.22 × 4%). The forecast for the risk-free rate over the coming years is 5%, giving a total required return of 10%.

Bank A has $10 billion of capital, and the management is reviewing the business plan for the coming years. Based on the internal management accounts, management is able to determine that the direct costs of the bank are normally around 60% of expected revenues, and taxes and other items absorb a further 20% of actual revenues. Bonuses are expected to be 5% of revenues, but this falls to zero if revenues fall below expectations by two standard deviations and caps out a maximum 10% if revenues exceed expectations by the same margin. Average return on capital has been 10%, or $1 billion.

Note that revenues here are stated net of loan losses; this puts the loan business onto a quasi-mark-to-market basis, ensuring that losses are accounted for in the same way that the trading business recognises losses: immediately, through the mark-to-market process.

By this means, the analysis of volatility can be focused on where it most counts: in the revenues of the bank, and Table 5.3 can be created from the information available. Starting at the bottom (net profit of $1 billion), one can then work up the central column (average year) to complete the model (in practice, more information is available about each individual line, and the model can be constructed accordingly). The revenues are then changed either side of the mean by ± one standard deviation (which is 10% of the mean) and then again by another standard deviation. The columns are then completed with the remaining information, assuming that non-bonus costs remain fixed, that bonuses range from 0% to 10% of revenues, as described above, and that taxes etc. are always 20% of revenues.

Note that the variation in revenues, in percentage terms, becomes magnified at the net profit level. This is because of the leverage caused mainly by the fixed costs, which remain constant over the range. Although the bonus number is even more variable in percentage terms (it changes by ± 100% versus the mean over the range shown above), it is much smaller than the fixed costs. If nothing else, this demonstrates very clearly the importance of a flexible cost base: the cost of providing the trading, branch and IT infrastructure is such that banks have a much higher degree of fixed costs than other industries, making them very susceptible to changes in revenues (remember that revenues are defined here as being net of loan losses).

If the bank meets the benchmark established, then the earnings should be $1 billion (RoC of 10%). This RoC should be achievable in future years as well, with any increase in earnings implying an increase in capital, and vice versa. In the model shown in Table 5.3, the bank is in line with that target.

Table 5.3 Revenue volatility model

	-2σ	-1σ	μ	$+1\sigma$	$+2\sigma$
Revenues	5333	6000	6667	7333	8000
Direct costs	4000	4000	4000	4000	4000
Bonuses	0	150	333	550	800
Taxes etc.	1067	1200	1333	1467	1600
Net profit	267	650	1000	1317	1600

The bank can now assess the riskiness of its profits stream as a function of revenue volatility. The standard deviation of revenues is approximately $667 million dollars; at the net profit line, this converts into a standard deviation of approximately $333 million dollars. The differences between the columns are not identical at the net profit line, as the different variability of the components leads to a non-linear net profit pattern, so an average over the full range is taken. In practice, given a sufficiently good series of management accounts, it may be possible to create a net profit distribution directly. However, the table here is more than sufficient to illustrate the concept, and even in practice building such a simple model is often the first step to educating management as to the magnitude of the risks they are facing.

This relationship between capital, RoC and volatility can be converted into a simple risk model: for every $1 of average revenues, the bank is prepared to accept a standard deviation in the net profit of the bank of 50 cents (667 divided by 333). In other words, the bank is happy with average earnings of $1 billion (a 10% return), and is 68% confident (one standard deviation implies approximately 68% certainty) that it can achieve a result between $650 million and $1317 million (one standard deviation either side of the mean). The bank is 95% confident that the result will be between $267 million and $1600 million (± approximately two standard deviations). Statistically speaking, if the bank never changed its capital level (and in the absence of inflation etc.) it will produce an annual result which is lower than $267 million or higher than $1600 million only once in every 20 years (5% of the time).

The model shown here operates under the assumption of the normal distribution—the statisticians will have already spotted this weakness. Various statistical refinements are available to adjust for the fact that the real world is not quite as simple as this, but using the normal distribution makes it easier to illustrate the concept at this stage.

EARNINGS-AT-RISK VERSUS VALUE-AT-RISK

In order to communicate its view of the acceptable level of risk to the managers on the front line, the bank may well express this in terms of revenue volatility ($1.33 billion, or twice the standard deviation of $667 million), as this is a number which is easy to comprehend. It may well use the term *earnings-at-risk* to describe this amount. However, in order to relate to a target return on capital, management may wish to convert this earnings-at-risk measure to a risk capital, or value-at-risk, measure (often also called economic capital, as seen in the previous chapter).

Note that the bank's capital is $10 billion, *not* $667 million (the standard deviation of revenues) or even $333 million (the standard deviation of profits). This is important: many people, when dealing with this concept, make the mistake of concluding that the total capital requirement should be $333 million (or perhaps $666 million or $999 million, depending on the confidence interval used). Remember that the expected return was generated in the first place off a particular level of capital, and changes in that capital level will affect the expected returns. For example, if the bank had less than $10 billion of capital, then the same percentage RoC would imply a lower actual dollar amount of earnings, and in order to maintain the same risk/return relationship, then the dollar amount of the standard deviation would also have to fall. Thus, if capital were only $5 billion, then a 10% RoC would result in average profits of $500 million with a standard deviation of $167 million (half of $333). Generating higher levels of earnings off a lower capital base would be very difficult to achieve, given the requirements to maintain certain capital levels imposed on banks.

A better way of regarding the relationship between earnings volatility and capital is to ask how much capital would be needed to ensure that the probable level of volatility is offset by risk-free earnings. How much capital, invested at a risk-free rate of, say, 5%, generates a return of $333 million per year? An investment of $6.66 billion at 5% will generate the required result, and thus it can be stated that, measured at this particular level of confidence, the economically required capital, or risk capital, is $6.66 billion. The relationship between earnings-at-risk and risk capital is therefore:

$$\text{Risk or economic capital} = \frac{\text{Earnings - at - risk}}{r}$$

where r is an interest rate (the risk-free rate, for example).

The parameters used in this model are not hard and fast—just as the decision as to confidence levels had a significant impact on the measure of risk capital in the previous chapter, so in this case is there considerable room for interpretation. The earnings-at-risk, for example, can be defined as anything from gross revenues right down to profit after tax, and the choice of interest rate can also be open to discussion (although this should always be a risk-free rate, as the intention behind this approach is to insure a shortfall against expectations by generating a guaranteed return). Empirical measures seem to suggest that annual revenue volatility, measured at a 95% confidence level and divided by the long-term risk-free rate, produces a good proxy for the levels of capital which banks actually have.

Another easy mistake to make here is to assume that the relationship between the standard deviation of profits and available capital is a fixed multiple (30 in this example). Assume that the bank could increase its profits by taking on more risk—say, to $1100 million on average and with a new standard deviation of $500 million. This implies a multiple of 20 if capital remains unchanged (10 billion divided by 500 million). Alternatively, if the multiple of 30 were to be fixed, then the bank's capital would have to increase to $15 billion to maintain the same ratio as before. But in that case, the RoC is going to fall to only 7.3% ($1.1 billion divided by $15 billion)! In either case, the relationship between RoC, capital and volatility changes.

The important aspect of the regression line introduced above is that it lets management weigh up the potential returns against the riskiness of those returns. The goal of management must be to perform above the regression line: that is to say, to produce a higher RoC for a given level of volatility, or a lower level of volatility for a given RoC. Banks which perform below the line are not returning their cost of capital, and will lose in stock market value when compared with their competitors.

USING THE MODEL AS A DECISION SUPPORT TOOL

This overall revenue/profit volatility model is the first step in building a risk capital model for the bank. Indeed, even without going so far as to build a risk capital model, the analysis can be used as a very useful decision support tool. At SBC, for example, we use these kind of distributions to look at the implied riskiness of achieving certain strategies. We will, for example, compare the projected revenues or profits for a planning period with the historical experience, as shown in Figure 5.2.

One has to be careful in interpreting this sort of analysis—a purely statistical approach does not say anything, for example, about changes in the business environment or in the bank's strategy, which could make statistically unlikely outcomes more possible, or expected outcomes riskier than they might seem at first sight. This is why it is emphasised that this is a decision support tool, with the emphasis on the word 'support': it is

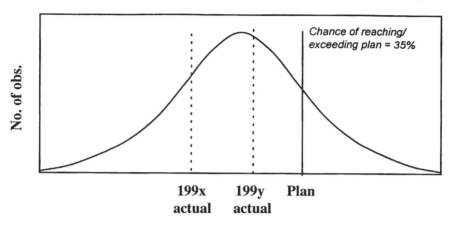

Figure 5.2   Using revenue distributions to support planning decisions

only one piece of information, albeit a very useful one, in making the planning decisions, and is certainly superior to comparing next year's budget with the actual performance of the last year or two.

RISK CAPITAL AS INSURANCE

Another way of looking at risk capital is to regard it as a form of insurance: it can provide a guarantee that the depositors of the bank will receive their funds back. In the definition introduced above, the amount of risk capital was set equal to the amount of capital which has to be invested in a safe instrument in order to insure the expected level of earnings. R. Merton and A. Perold[4] have shown that this insurance is provided in three descending tranches:

1. 'Normal' insurance, provided in the form of equity capital and/or parent guarantees (in either case, the shareholders bear any losses). The cost of this insurance is the excess return over the risk-free rate which the shareholders require from their investment in stock.
2. 'Disaster' insurance, provided by the holders of junior debt. The cost of this insurance is the excess yield which the noteholders require over the risk-free rate.
3. 'Catastrophe' insurance, provided by the depositors. In the final instance, it is the depositors who bear the residual risk not covered by equity and junior debt. It is hardest to ascertain the cost at this level, and most depositors are probably not aware of the fact that they are selling insurance! However, in an open market it might be possible to deduce this as the difference between the interest rate offered on customer deposits covered by

governmental guarantees (deposit insurance) and that offered on similar deposits not backed by an insurance program.

Unfortunately, whilst the approach does help to explain the role of capital and to define its cost, it does not provide an easy way of defining how much the insurance is worth for individual assets or businesses—this is like knowing that your household contents insurance costs you $500 a year, but you have no idea what the coverage is on individual items.

INTEGRATING EARNINGS AT RISK INTO THE OVERALL CAPITAL FRAMEWORK

It has already been noted that one cannot simply scale the revenue volatility and state that total capital must be a multiple thereof. Indeed, in Chapter 1 the role of capital was defined as a buffer against future, unidentified, even relatively improbable losses, whilst still leaving the bank able to operate at the same level of capacity. An extreme example helps to illustrate this point.

Imagine a bank similar to Bank A in the example above, but where the revenue volatility is even more pronounced. This bank is confident that it can earn 10% on average, but it can easily produce a loss in a particular year. If its regulatory capital requirement were exactly equal to the $10 billion available capital, then if the bank made a loss it would not be able to continue to expect to earn 10% on average, as it would have to scale down its size of operations so as to fall back within the regulatory limits (as the loss would mean that the available capital fell below the regulatory capital requirement). This would almost certainly mean revising its business plans downwards, leading in turn to a loss of revenue. The bank would then find it harder to produce higher earnings in the next period to compensate shareholders for the loss (remember that the bank has to produce an average 10% on the value of the original investment).

The same is true in less extreme cases: a bank may be dependent on a certain level of retained earnings in order to finance future expansion. Or it may need to meet market expectations in terms of either reported earnings or dividends. Thus the earnings at risk of the bank must be the amount of expected earnings which the management of the bank is willing to forego in any one period, within a given level of confidence, without causing a change in business plans.

This may partly explain the conundrum of higher capital levels examined in Chapter 1—the management of banks wish to be able to maintain a certain level of dividend so as to signal their confidence in future earnings, and at the same time do not wish to fall below their regulatory capital requirement, as this would imply a curtailment of business volumes, and thus the earnings-at-risk is set as a kind of 'safety buffer'. Many banks will be content with a 95% confidence level, but more conservative banks will require a higher level of confidence. A factor to be considered is also the fact that the past is not always an accurate guide to the future, which again influences banks to err on the side of caution.

A point to watch out for is the distinction between equity and capital here: it has previously been stated that the exact definition of capital is not important for the techniques described in this book, as the relationship between capital and equity can be scaled:

$$\text{RoE} \times \frac{\text{equity}}{\text{capital}} = \text{RoC}$$

However, lost earnings are deducted entirely from equity, not from any subordinated debt which might also be included in the definition of capital. In all of the above examples, it was assumed that equity equates to capital (simply to keep the examples clear). Imagine instead that the bank has a limit of 20% as to the amount of debt which it can use to contribute to capital (this may be an internally imposed limit, driven by management's assessment of the amount of debt it can place at a reasonable cost, or a regulatory limit), and its regulatory capital requirement is $11 250 million.

The risk capital requirement previously calculated (1 standard deviation of profits, or $333 million, divided by the risk-free rate, giving $6.66 billion) cannot be scaled up according to the ratio of capital to equity, as the earnings volatility goes entirely at the expense of the equity holders. The regulatory capital, on the other hand, can be scaled up, based on the allowable proportion of debt in the total capital calculation. Table 5.4 demonstrates this.

WHAT TIME PERIOD TO USE?

The model described above defined revenue volatility in terms of the standard deviation of annual revenues, building a model which also provided a distribution of earnings, again expressed in annual terms. This is a difficult measure to use on an ongoing basis, as management will want

Table 5.4 Scaling regulatory and risk capital/equity

	Capital	Equity
Regulatory		
• Requirement	11 250	9000
• Available	12 500	10 000
Surplus	1250	1000
Economic/risk		
• Requirement	6660	6660
• Available	10 000	10 000
Surplus	3340	3340

to use a more frequent measurement to see whether they are on target or not. The stock market also sees earnings on a more regular basis—at least semi-annually, and in many countries quarterly. Also, on a practical note, a time series of annual revenues which contained enough data points (at least 12–15 are recommended) to provide an analysis would, firstly, take an inordinately long time to put together and, secondly, would run the risk of paradigm shifts during the period breaking the series (changes in organisation, environment etc.). Thus it may be necessary to convert the model into one which uses shorter time periods, such as months or quarters.

Also, when applying the model retrospectively to benchmark the bank against competitors, it is advisable to use the historical distribution of quarterly or semi-annual revenues/earnings so as to obtain a sufficiently large sample of recent data, which will need to be converted into annual numbers for the sake of comparison. Finally, when setting top-down targets based on budgets and business plans, it may be necessary to convert annual targets into shorter time periods, so as to provide a benchmark which can be referred to frequently. Making the assumption that revenues in one period are independent of revenues in the adjacent periods (admittedly a brave assumption), this conversion can be performed using the 'square-root-of-time' technique already encountered.

For example, in the case of Bank A, we can convert the annual revenue to quarterly revenue as follows:

Mean	6667 million annually	= 1666 million quarterly
Std deviation	667 million annually	= 333 million quarterly

It is probably not worth going to a more frequent measurement interval than quarterly, unless this can be produced with no extra effort (at SBC, we produce monthly management accounts for the Group and it is therefore easy to derive the monthly volatilities). Except in trading businesses, where even more frequent measurement might be desirable, more frequent than monthly would definitely be a case of overkill, and apparent volatility may be created by the nature of accounting routines (interest earnings may often be booked only once a month, for example, even though they technically accrue smoothly over time).

SUMMARY

Using the regression of betas against revenue volatility shown in Figure 5.1, it is possible for banks to build models of their expected revenues and thus earnings, and to compare this against the return which the market expects given that level of volatility. An understanding of the relationship between average returns and the volatility of those returns is fundamental to ensuring that the bank's strategy is consistent with the market's expectations in terms of reward. Chapter 6 expands this model to provide a business-specific risk capital model for use within the bank, both as a performance measure and a tool to assess the relative value of alternative strategies.

Whilst the calculations demonstrated in this chapter may not be perfect—a number of assumptions and simplifications have to be made—some broad measures can be derived which enable us to benchmark results and strategies. However, this information, useful as it is, cannot produce a routinely formulaic answer to the appropriate level of capital for a particular bank—it is only one of many inputs which the management of the bank must take into account.

ENDNOTES

1. The CAPM was originally published in two classic articles: 'Capital asset prices: A theory of market equilibrium under conditions of risk', W. F. Sharpe, *Journal of Finance,* September 1964; 'Security prices, risk and maximal gains from diversification', J. Lintner; *Journal of Finance,* December 1965
2. This assertion is examined in more detail in Chapter 9.
3. I am grateful to my colleague, Patrick Freymond, for this derivation of the

usual beta equation—we have not seen it in any text book, but it is much easier to understand than the usual definition. Its derivation is simple:

$$\beta = \frac{\text{Cov}_{(i,m)}}{\sigma_m^2}$$

Since $\text{Corr}_{i,m} = \dfrac{\text{Cov}_{(i,m)}}{\sigma_i . \sigma_m}$ then $\text{Cov}_{(i,m)} = \text{Corr}_{(i,m)} . \sigma_i . \sigma_m$

Substituting, we get $\beta = \dfrac{\text{Corr}_{(i,m)} . \sigma_i . \sigma_m}{\sigma_m^2}$

Then dividing by σ_m we get $\beta = \text{Corr}_{(i,m)} \dfrac{\sigma_i}{\sigma_m}$

4. 'Management of risk capital in financial firms', Robert C. Merton and André F. Perold in *Financial Services: Perspectives and Challenges,* ed. Samuel Hayes, Harvard Business School Press, 1993.

6

Earnings-volatility-based
Approaches

Chapter 5 established a basic model for capital, which suggested that:

Risk capital = amount required which, invested at the risk-free rate, covers the potential downside in earnings.

This model provides a good rule of thumb for management when determining the proper amount of capital for the bank as a whole, but will it work at the level of individual businesses?

This chapter examines an approach which attempts to answer this question; this can be classified as an 'earnings at risk' approach, in contrast to the 'value-at-risk' approach seen in Chapter 4. Like the top-down model demonstrated in the previous chapter, the definition of risk capital or economic capital is derived from the observed volatility of earnings. After examining the methodology for calculating earnings at risk, various models for converting this into a risk-capital measure are introduced. Finally, the chapter concludes with a look at the limitations of the earnings-volatility-based approach to risk capital, and compares it with the asset-volatility approach set out in Chapter 4.

The examples used here refer mainly to businesses within a bank. At Swiss Bank Corporation, our primary organisational units are Business Areas. These are similar to the strategic business units (SBUs) of the management literature of the 1980's (Porter's *Competitive Strategy* etc.). A Business Area has a clearly defined, distinct strategy, and could conceivably exist as an independent business, although different business areas may share common service providers or distribution networks. Retail banking, private banking and corporate finance are examples of business areas. When the text below refers to 'businesses', organisational units similar to SBC's Business Areas are meant. However, the techniques can be applied to different organisational forms and levels as well.

BASIC RISK CAPITAL MODEL

The basic model which underlies earnings-volatility-based approaches is a definition of earnings-at-risk (EAR) using some measure of the extent to which revenues or earnings deviate either side of the mean.

A generic definition of EAR is thus:

$$EAR = k\sigma_r$$

where k is a constant, and (σ_r) refers to the standard deviation of the revenues or earnings of the bank or business. In plain English, all this says is that earnings-at-risk are defined as a certain number (k) of standard deviations of the distribution of earnings. The generic model can use revenues, contribution (some measure of revenues, less direct costs, for example), net profit (before or after tax) etc.—the choice depends very much on the structure and reliability of management accounts (it is much easier to attribute revenues to businesses than it is to attribute net profit, as any allocation of overheads will of necessity be somewhat arbitrary) as well as on the signals which management wishes to send (as examined in more detail in Chapter 10).

THEOBANK INC.

A theoretical bank illustrates the calculations and concepts demonstrated in this chapter. Theobank Inc. is a universal bank, involved in private banking and asset management, in retail banking, in commercial banking and in investment banking. This may seem like a broad spread of activities, but it is exactly what many big European universal banks do. Other banks may not be involved in all of these activities, but the techniques demonstrated are equally applicable to banks with a smaller spread of business. To keep the examples easy, it is assumed that all of Theobank's balance sheet, revenues and costs are in US dollars.

Figure 6.1 shows the organisation structure of Theobank Inc.

Table 6.1 gives summary financial information in respect of the different businesses (it is assumed that all business have their own internal operations and technology functions, or alternatively that the costs of these functions are fully allocated across the businesses).

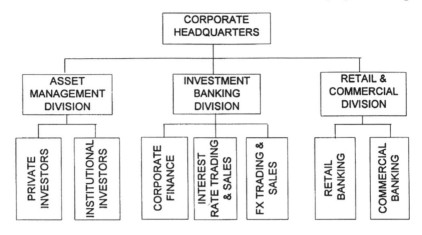

Figure 6.1   Theobank Inc Organisation

To keep the example simple, it is assumed that Theobank Inc. has no Tier 2 capital: it is entirely supported by equity, and thus 'capital' and 'equity' are interchangeable in this context.

Adopting the top-down approach to earnings volatility shown in the previous chapter, the volatility of the revenues of the bank as a whole is a good starting point.

Table 6.2 shows the total revenues of Theobank over the last 24 months, repeated in Figure 6.2 as a bar chart where the horizontal axis

Table 6.1   Theobank Inc financial summary

	Average annual revenues	Operating costs	Credit provisions	Taxes etc.	Net profit	Regulatory capital
Private investors	1200	700	30	120	350	1400
Inst'l investors	360	200	0	30	130	500
Corp. finance	120	50	20	10	40	400
Interset rates	156	70	0	16	70	600
FX	84	30	0	14	40	100
Retail banking	480	300	70	20	90	1200
Commercial banking	240	200	20	0	20	1000
Corporate HQ	0	30	10	0	−40	500
Theobank Inc.	**2640**	**1580**	**150**	**210**	**700**	**5700**
Total equity (Tier 1)						**6000**
Return on equity						**11.7%**

shows the size of the earnings in buckets and the vertical axis measures the number of months in each bucket: this gives an immediate feel for the shape of the distribution. Superimposed on the bar chart is the normal distribution curve, and one can see that the bar chart is a reasonably good fit to the statistical distribution (statisticians would actually say that it is a negatively skewed distribution—more on non-normal distributions can be found in the appendix to this chapter). The mean of these revenues is $220 million, with a standard deviation of $25.6 million. Recall that Theobank has average annual earnings of $700 million and capital of $6 billion—the revenue volatility is really very small in comparison to either the net profit or the capital base. This can be observed in the case of real banks: the capital held by the banks is a substantial multiple of the potential earnings volatility, if measured by statistical techniques such as the standard deviation.

Of course, the number calculated in Table 6.2 is the *monthly* standard deviation, which cannot be compared with the *annual* earnings. In a normal world, the series of variables in a distribution (such as the distribution of revenues shown in Figure 6.2) are independent of each other, and in such cases the monthly standard deviation is converted into an annual number by using the 'square-root-of-time' rule already demonstrated. Multiplying 25.56 by $\sqrt{12}$ gives an annualised standard deviation of $88.5 million.

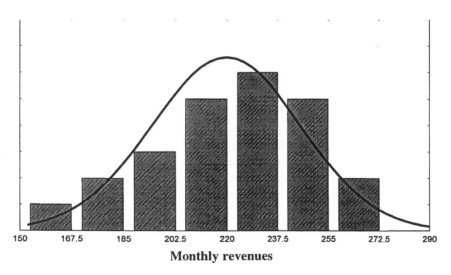

Figure 6.2   Theobank: distribution of revenues

Table 6.2   Theobank's revenues

Month	Revenue	Month	Revenue
t−24	237.00	t−12	184.00
t−23	240.00	t−11	209.00
t−22	162.00	t−10	237.00
t−21	195.00	t−9	225.00
t−20	204.00	t−8	223.00
t−19	190.00	t−7	228.00
t−18	216.00	t−6	245.00
t−17	208.00	t−5	235.00
t−16	213.00	t−4	256.00
t−15	249.00	t−3	256.00
t−14	243.00	t−2	200.00
t−13	182.00	t−1	243.00
Mean	**220.00**		
S.D.	**25.56**		

(This assumption of normality is often the only practical approach: calculating the actual annual standard deviation can only be performed by looking at a sufficiently long series of annual revenues. Such a series is however grossly distorted by the change in environment which occurs over such a long period—changes in regulation and business mix, for example. We are interested in the bank as it currently stands, and thus have to use more recent data. This is a limitation we just have to accept.)

One standard deviation implies a confidence interval of around two thirds: that is to say, annual revenues will be no more than $88.5 million either side of a mean of $2640 million two thirds of the time (the mean revenues are annualised simply by multiplying by the number of time periods—in this case 12). This level of confidence is probably too low for most managements, and so a higher level of two or three standard deviations is likely to be chosen. Using three standard deviations gives $265 million (88.5 × 3), and one can state that under this definition EAR is therefore $265 million.

However, such a simple, unadjusted number for EAR can send out the wrong kinds of signals to staff. Whilst it may make sense to those who have done the calculations, it is a number to which many people have difficulty relating. Theobank, with capital of $6 billion and average earnings of $700 million, has a return on capital of 11.7% (Table 6.1). If

EAR is taken as a definition of risk capital, the return on risk capital bears no relation to the actual RoC:

$$\text{Return on risk capital} = \frac{700}{265} = 264\%!!!!!$$

One can imagine how staff will react when they are told their target is to achieve, say, a 300% return on risk capital! The alternative is to increase the number of standard deviations—but this produces equally ludicrous signals: using 40 standard deviations produces an intuitively sensible 20% return (700 divided by 40 times 88.5), but how does one explain a confidence interval of this size?

The conundrum has its roots in the fact that, as has been already observed, the revenue volatility of a bank is only a fraction of the capital which banks have to hold. An approach is required to account for this relationship, in order to produce a management tool which can be meaningfully applied (capital allocation should *not* remain just an academic exercise).

There are three easy models which can be used to convert the EAR number into a meaningful risk capital measure, and all of these will be examined in turn (there are probably a lot more than three, but most will turn out to be variations on the same themes). Before looking at these models, however, the EAR for individual businesses must be calculated—once calculated, it can be slotted into any one of the models. Indeed, the calculation of the EAR is where most of the work has to be done—once calculated, the application of the three risk capital models can be done in a few seconds, and some banks may wish to use more than one measure.

In calculating the earnings volatility of individual businesses, we very quickly run into a problem which must be addressed: how does the impact of diversification of earnings across different businesses affect the relationship between the earnings volatility of individual businesses and that of the bank as a whole?

The effect of diversification on earnings is one of the cornerstones of modern financial theory (and practice, for that matter), and although it is not intended here to repeat the corporate finance textbooks, a brief exegesis is warranted for the reader who is not familiar with the concept. Those readers who do not need to refresh their memories on this subject may skip the text box.

The traditional way to compare the riskiness of two different assets is to use the standard deviation of their returns. Usually, these returns are expressed in percentages, to eliminate the effect of size (a $5 return on a $50 dollar stock is the same in percentage terms as a $10 return on a $100 stock), but this is not absolutely necessary. This example uses percentage returns, but elsewhere in the text absolute numbers are used.

Imagine that we have two stocks: Wizzo Inc. and Boring Inc. Wizzo is a pretty exciting company, but the returns on its stock are rather volatile. Boring, on the other hand, is what its name implies: a rather steady plodder with uninspiring but steady returns. The returns over the last four years are shown in Box 1.

Box 1	Returns on Wizzo and Boring	
	Wizzo Inc	Boring Inc
Year1	20%	−5%
Year 2	−10%	5%
Year 3	30%	6%
Year 4	40%	10%

The average returns on each stock were:

Wizzo Inc.: $(20\% - 10\% + 40\% + 30\%) \div 4 = 20\%$
Boring Inc.: $(-5\% + 5\% + 6\% + 10\%) \div 4 = 4\%$

and the standard deviations are:

Wizzo Inc.:   21.6%
Boring Inc.:   6.4%

What is interesting here is what happens when we add the two stocks together to form a portfolio. If we put half of our money in Wizzo, and half in Boring, our expected return will be the weighted average of the two stocks:

$(0.5 \times 20\%) + (0.5 \times 4\%) = 12\%$

But what will the riskiness of the portfolio be? One might intuitively suggest that it would be the weighted average of the standard deviations of the two stocks, namely:

$(0.5 \times 21.6\%) + (0.5 \times 6.4\%) = 14\%$

But this is not what happens. To work out what the standard deviation of the combined portfolio would be, let us first look at the combined returns in each year, and then re-calculate the standard deviation of this new data series, as shown in Box 2.

Box 2	Returns on combined portfolio			
	Wizzo Inc	Boring Inc	Portfolio (50% each)	Variance of portfolio
Year 1	20%	–5%	7.5%	0.2025%
Year 2	–10%	5%	–2.5%	2.1025%
Year 3	30%	6%	18.0%	0.3600%
Year 4	40%	10%	25.0%	1.6900%
Average	20%	4%	12%	
Std deviation				12.05%

The average return on the combined portfolio is 12%, as we would have expected:

$$(7.5\% - 2.5\% + 18\% + 25\%) \div 4 = 12\%$$

But the standard deviation is actually just over 12%,[1] not the 14% we expected. Why is this? The answer lies in the concept of *diversification*— something most bankers understand intuitively, but it is also worthwhile understanding the statistical underpinning. Because Wizzo and Boring are not perfectly *correlated*—that is to say, they do not move in tandem—there is a dampening effect which occurs when we add them together. What is particularly important is that the benefits of diversification can be felt even if the assets in question are positively correlated, as long as they are not *perfectly* correlated. (Incidentally, the correlation of Wizzo and Boring is +0.2).

The whole edifice of modern finance is built on this remarkable observation—the riskiness of a portfolio consisting of a combination of assets is nearly always lower than (and never more than equal to) the sum of the riskiness of the component assets.

EARNINGS-AT-RISK FOR INDIVIDUAL BUSINESSES

Repeating the calculation shown in Table 6.2, the standard deviation of the revenues of the individual businesses within Theobank can be calculated. Table 6.3 shows the distribution of revenues over the last 24 months (analogous to Table 6.2), broken down by business.

The first thing to notice is the impact of diversification: the standard deviation of the bank's revenues is much less than the sum of the standard deviations of the three divisions, which are in turn less than the sum of the standard deviations of the component businesses.

Table 6.3 Theobank revenues by business

	t-1	t-2	t-3	t-4	t-5	t-6	t-7	t-8	t-9	t-10	t-11	t-12	t-13	t-14	t-15	t-16	t-17	t-18	t-19	t-20	t-21	t-22	t-23	t-24	Mean	SD
Private investors	104	103	108	106	103	102	97	92	94	103	102	96	98	101	103	105	102	101	97	93	94	102	99	95	100	4.39
Inst'l investors	42	42	39	37	41	38	34	36	35	32	33	31	29	27	27	24	26	21	23	23	21	22	18	19	30	7.67
Asset mgt	**146**	**145**	**147**	**143**	**144**	**140**	**131**	**128**	**129**	**135**	**135**	**127**	**127**	**128**	**130**	**129**	**128**	**122**	**120**	**116**	**115**	**124**	**117**	**114**	**130**	**10.14**
Corp. finance	13	5	10	6	4	9	17	15	6	13	5	7	6	17	6	13	3	18	14	5	9	7	20	12	10	5.01
Interest rates	15	(7)	29	25	18	22	12	15	20	18	(4)	(2)	17	26	12	17	7	7	-5	15	11	-15	24	35	13	12.33
FX	5	(2)	8	17	14	12	9	1	6	14	8	(6)	(4)	14	20	3	9	14	-3	3	4	-12	14	20	7	8.42
Investment bkg	**33**	**-4**	**47**	**48**	**36**	**43**	**38**	**31**	**32**	**45**	**20**	**-3**	**0**	**48**	**52**	**28**	**29**	**39**	**6**	**23**	**24**	**-20**	**58**	**67**	**30**	**21.44**
Retail banking	42	39	40	42	38	43	39	41	43	38	36	40	38	44	43	37	35	38	44	43	37	39	43	38	40	2.70
Commercial banking	22	20	22	23	17	19	20	23	21	19	18	20	17	23	24	19	16	17	20	22	19	19	22	18	20	2.25
Retail/comm.	**64**	**59**	**62**	**65**	**55**	**62**	**59**	**64**	**64**	**57**	**54**	**60**	**55**	**67**	**67**	**56**	**51**	**55**	**64**	**65**	**56**	**58**	**65**	**56**	**60**	**4.66**
Theobank Inc.	**243**	**200**	**256**	**256**	**235**	**245**	**228**	**223**	**225**	**237**	**209**	**184**	**182**	**243**	**249**	**213**	**208**	**216**	**190**	**204**	**195**	**162**	**240**	**237**	**220**	**25.56**

The second important point to notice is that these are *monthly* revenues. Theobank wishes to base risk capital on three standard deviations of its *annual* earnings, so the 'square-root-of-time' rule is applied. Table 6.4 shows the EAR for each business defined as three annual standard deviations (three times the monthly standard deviation, multiplied by $\sqrt{12}$ to annualise it).

Notice that the impact of diversification on the total has not yet been taken into account: the sum of the EAR of the different businesses is much greater than the EAR of the bank as a whole. The difference is shown in Table 6.4 as a 'diversification credit' at the different levels of consolidation.

DEALING WITH DIVERSITY (1): DIVERSIFICATION ACROSS BUSINESSES

Whilst it is useful to be able to look at the EAR on an 'undiversified' basis, the management of Theobank might wish to go further than this, and calculate the EAR on a fully diversified basis. This is quite an important adjustment: given that the sum of the EARs of the individual businesses greatly exceeds overall EAR, failing to account for diversification could result in sub-optimal capital allocation. Indeed, a highly volatile business might actually have the effect of *dampening* the overall volatility of the bank: viewed on its own, it might look unattractive, but viewed in context of the bank as a whole, it could be a surprisingly attractive business.

Table 6.4 Earnings-at-risk of Theobank's businesses

Private investors	45.66
Inst'l investors	79.74
Diversification credit	*− 20.04*
Asset mgt	**105.36**
Corp. finance	52.10
Interest rates	128.16
FX	87.54
Diversification credit	*− 44.97*
Investment bkg	**222.83**
Retail banking	28.09
Commercial banking	23.34
Diversification credit	*− 2.97*
Retail/comm.	**48.45**
Diversification credit	*− 110.96*
Theobank Inc.	**265.68**

A simple way to do this is to calculate the correlation of each business with the total and then multiply the EAR by that multiplication factor. Table 6.5 shows the correlation factors of each business, multiplied by the undiversified EAR of each. Note that the diversification credit is now spread across all of the component businesses, and the sum of these now equals the EAR of the bank as a whole.

The problem here is the variability of the impact of diversification: if the mix of the businesses is changed, then there will be a change in the overall correlation of each business with the total, and the result could be a different level of overall volatility to that which management intended.

For example, the corporate finance business of Theobank has a correlation factor of 0.27 and an undiversified EAR of $52.1 million, giving a diversified EAR of $14.07 million. Changes in the other businesses—without any changes in corporate finance—would result in a changed correlation factor for corporate finance, and thus a changed diversified EAR number (of course, the EAR of the bank as a whole will have changed as well). Corporate finance might end up with a new correlation factor of 0.54, implying a doubling in its diversified EAR measure to $28.1 million. If the bonus pool of the employees of this business were driven off this factor, they might be rather upset by this!

Table 6.5   Adjusting for diversification

	Correlation factor	Earnings at risk	Diversified EAR
Private investors	0.38	45.66	17.32
Inst'l investors	0.36	79.74	28.44
Diversification credit			*0.00*
Asset mgt	**0.43**	**105.36**	**45.76**
Corp. finance	0.27	52.10	14.07
Interest rates	0.88	128.16	112.20
FX	0.84	87.54	73.58
Diversification credit			*0.00*
Investment bkg	**0.90**	**222.83**	**199.84**
Retail banking	0.34	28.09	9.51
Commercial banking	0.45	23.34	10.57
Diversification credit			*0.00*
Retail/comm.	**0.41**	**48.45**	**20.08**
Diversification credit			*0.00*
Theobank Inc.	**1.00**	**265.68**	**265.68**

DEALING WITH DIVERSITY (2): THE MARGINAL IMPACT OF INDIVIDUAL BUSINESSES

The problem with the change in mix affecting the correlations has been aptly demonstrated in the theoretical literature; R. Merton and A. Perold[2] argue that the correct measure of risk capital is actually the *marginal* risk capital required by an individual business, and since risk capital is derived from EAR, this can be applied to the revenues as well.

To calculate this, the time series of Theobank's revenues is restated, removing in turn each business or division from the series. The standard deviation of Theobank is then recalculated without the missing business, and the difference between this and the original standard deviation can be seen as the marginal impact of each business on the bank as a whole. The result is given in Table 6.6: it can be seen that the marginal EAR is even lower than the fully diversified EAR.

Note also that a diversification affect appears again in consolidating the divisions, but that there is also a substantial portion of EAR which is not allocated to any business.

The difference between the undiversified, diversified and marginal

Table 6.6   Marginal earnings-at-risk

	Undiversified EAR	Diversified EAR	Marginal EAR
Private investors	45.66	17.32	13.46
Inst'l investors	79.74	28.44	16.66
Diversification credit	*−20.04*	*0.00*	*−4.52*
Asset mgt	**105.36**	**45.76**	**25.60**
Corp. finance	52.10	14.07	8.93
Interest rates	128.16	112.20	98.06
FX	87.54	73.58	66.38
Diversification credit	*−44.97*	*0.00*	*−29.31*
Investment bkg	**222.83**	**199.84**	**144.05**
Retail banking	28.09	9.51	7.98
Commercial banking	23.34	10.57	9.52
Diversification credit	*−2.97*	*0.00*	*−7.98*
Retail/comm.	**48.45**	**20.08**	**9.52**
Diversification credit	*−110.96*	*0.00*	*86.51*

EAR measures is very much like the old accounting chestnut of whether to use fully allocated costs. If costs are fully allocated, then additional marginal transactions may appear unattractive, as they do not cover all costs. But many of these costs are fixed, and the addition of a further transaction has no impact on them. Therefore using a fully costed system can lead to missed opportunities. On the other hand, if the costs are not fully allocated, then there is a risk of every transaction being priced at the margin, with the result that insufficient contribution is earned to cover all costs.

The trick, of course—as all wise cost accountants learned long ago—is that there is no single correct answer, and that one uses different measures to support different decisions in different circumstances. The characteristics and uses of the three different measures are summarised in Table 6.7.

Table 6.7 Different measures of earnings-at-risk

Measure	Characteristics	Typical uses
Undiversified	Total EAR is less than the sum of the EAR of the parts	As this measure looks at the riskiness of each business or sub-unit independently, it is useful for performance measurement (bonus pools etc.)
Diversified	Total EAR is exactly equal to the sum of the EAR of the parts	This measure is not suitable for performance measurement, as the results for one business can be affected by changes in other businesses. However, as it correctly reflects the riskiness of the bank as a whole, it needs to be taken into account when making capital allocation decisions.
Marginal	Total EAR is greater than the sum of the EAR of the parts	This measure is not suitable for performance measurement, as it again can be influenced by changes exogenous to the business being measured. However, it is very useful for marginal decisions, such as whether to enter or exit a particular business.

At SBC, we believe that it is important to look at all of these measures (especially the undiversified and diversified measures), and we compare changes in performance measured by each. These measures are used primarily to support strategic decisions (which businesses do we wish to invest in), and it is at this level that earnings-volatility-based models are most useful.

THE BASIC RORAC MODEL

Having determined the possible definition of EAR, we now turn our attention to the possible models which can be used to convert these numbers into some sort of performance measure. The term return on risk-adjusted capital (RORAC) is used to describe these, as the risk adjustment in all cases occurs in the denominator.

RORAC (I)

A very simple, pragmatic approach is to spread the available equity of the bank as a whole across the businesses, in the proportion of their relative EARs. This can be done using either the undiversified or the diversified measure.

$$\frac{\text{return}}{\text{total available equity} \times \dfrac{\text{EAR of business}}{\text{EAR of the bank}}}$$

This is certainly intuitive, as it ensures that the calculation at the bank-wide level is equal to the bank's return on equity, which is the ratio we are trying to optimise. However, it suffers from two major limitations:

1. It spreads any surplus equity over the businesses, ignoring capital *required* by replacing it with capital *available*. This will not aid the bank in achieving optimal capital levels.
2. The return calculated for any one business is dependent on changes in the overall EAR of the bank, which may be generated by other businesses.

Thus the criticism of interdependence raised against the diversified EAR measure above is here encountered twice: once because changes in the available equity affect the denominator, and again because changes in the EAR of other businesses likewise affect the denominator.

RORAC (II)

This model treats regulatory capital as a cost of doing business, and sets the risk capital as equal to the annual earnings-at-risk:

$$\frac{\text{return} - \text{opportunity cost of regulatory capital}}{\text{earnings - at - risk}}$$

The opportunity cost can be the risk-free rate, the actual cost of capital, or some hurdle rate.

Using the risk-free rate will result in infinite risk-adjusted returns if one invests in a risk-free asset (as both the regulatory capital number and the risk capital are zero—the latter because a risk-free asset, by definition, has no volatility in its returns). The model implies that all of the bank's equity is invested in risk-free assets, or alternatively that the assets of the businesses can be refinanced in full at the risk-free rate. Thus the numerator of the equation effectively gives returns in excess of the risk-free rate, divided by the risk entered into to obtain those returns.

Using the cost of capital sets the hurdle rate higher, as any business which earns less than the cost of the regulatory capital absorbed will report a negative result. The beauty of this variation is that it is totally compatible with the concept of shareholder value analysis (see Chapter 9), which teaches that the net present value of free cash flows, discounted at the bank's cost of capital, must be positive if wealth is to be generated for the shareholders. Since regulatory capital is essentially a deduction from free cash flow (because it represents equity which cannot be returned to shareholders nor invested elsewhere) for as long as it is locked into current transactions, using the cost of capital in the equation gives an easy guide as to whether businesses are generating value (the model reports a positive return) or destroying value (negative returns). The answer, however, is not always as black and white as this, as factors such as the difference between the stock market's measure of return and the internal return-on-book-value-of-equity, or the influence of future investment on current year's profit, may have a distorting effect.

Applying the model to Theobank as a whole, using 5% as a risk-free rate and 10% as the cost of equity (remember that, to keep things simple, it was assumed that Theobank's capital base is 100% equity), gives the following RORACs:

$$\text{using risk-free rate} = \frac{700 - (5700 \times 5\%)}{266} = 156\%$$

$$\text{using cost of capital} = \frac{700 - (5700 \times 10\%)}{266} = 49\%$$

As Theobank is actually earning a return of nearly 12% on its equity, it is clearly generating value if its capital costs are only 10%, which is why both RORAC calculations show very positive returns.

A final variation is to use an even higher target rate. This can be particularly useful when a bank is currently earning much less than it aspires to, but can run the risk that business opportunities which create value get turned down because they do not make the target rate.

RORAC (III)

The final variation on the RORAC model uses the concept of risk-free investment as an insurance against earnings volatility. This model asks 'how much capital must I invest, at the risk-free rate, in order to generate a return sufficient to offset the potential downside risk in earnings?'. In the case of Theobank, the earnings-at-risk are $266 million. In order to produce a return of $266, a risk-free investment yielding 5% in the amount of $5320 million would need to be made.

In the case of this variation of the RORAC model risk capital is redefined as:

$$\text{risk capital} = \frac{\text{earnings-at-risk}}{\text{risk-free rate}} = \frac{266}{5\%} = 5320$$

The RORAC is defined as the return divided by the risk capital.

$$\frac{700}{5320} = 13.1\%$$

This approach to RORAC is probably superior to the others, as:

1. It produces returns which are intuitively sensible.
2. It puts earnings in relation to capital invested, a relationship with which most people are comfortable.
3. It allows businesses to be measured independently (the measure is not affected by changes in the risk capital of other businesses, if the 'undiversified' measure of earnings at risk is used).

As with RORAC (II), the rate used can either be the risk-free rate, the cost of capital or a target rate of return.

Selecting target rates for different businesses

An argument has raged amongst consultants, and between consultants and their clients, as to whether the same cost of capital should be applied to all business opportunities. At the end of the day, it is up to management to decide what suits their philosophy best. When launching the focus on RoE more than a decade ago, Lloyds Bank apparently accepted the same target RoE for all businesses: not because it was correct, but because it was easier to implement and communicate.

However, one must recognise that the business of banking—taking in deposits and making loans—was much more homogenous in the early 1980s than it is today. The regression analysis shown in Chapter 5 clearly demonstrates that different segments of the banking industry have different costs of capital, according to their riskiness. This cannot be ignored when allocating capital in a multi-disciplined bank. At SBC, we expect much higher returns from our investment banking businesses than from private banking, as the risks are also much higher. Indeed, using the same hurdle rate would effectively induce us to putting all of our capital into investment banking, at the expense of highly profitable but less volatile businesses.

LIMITATIONS OF THE EARNINGS VOLATILITY MODEL

There are a number of drawbacks to the model demonstrated in this chapter:

1. The assumption of normality was made to derive measures such as the standard deviation. In reality, earnings are not normally distributed, but exhibit a number of statistical complications. Most of these can be dealt with (see statistical appendix at the end of this chapter), the rest we just have to live with. Whatever model is used to approximate risk, certain statistical simplifications will be necessary, on the basis that the only reasonable guide to the future is the past. If this is rejected, then we cannot make any statements as to how much capital we think we are going to need and we should just cross our fingers and pray!

2. The approach is ex-post: it tells something about the risks already encountered, but assumes going forward that the bank continues to face the same risks. The technique fails to capture sudden changes in riskiness: the risks run by Mr Leeson at Barings escalated very suddenly over a short period of time, and any model based on past earnings volatility (even if he had reported his earnings correctly) would have failed to pick up this quantum jump until it was too late. The asset-volatility approach examined in Chapter 4 gets round this problem (to a certain degree) by modelling the risks ex-ante.

3. The model proves no clues as to how to control the risk capital: it may tell us that a business is running a great deal of risk (high volatility), but other than a broad instruction to those responsible to 'reduce their risks', there are no levers management can pull to reduce the volatility.

However, the earnings-volatility approach is useful for at least three applications:

1. It lends itself very well to ex-post performance-related compensation measures such as bonus schemes, as it correctly measures returns over a period against the riskiness of those same returns.
2. It relates well to the position of the bank as a whole in the market i.e. to its cost of capital and, most importantly, to the concept of shareholder value analysis.
3. When making marginal decisions (whether to enter or exit a business), the technique can be used to determine the marginal impact on the bank as a whole. Businesses which by themselves have quite a high volatility may actually have a dampening effect on the volatility of the bank as a whole, contributing to a lower cost of capital.

Although a major limitation is that the approach does not indicate how to steer risks, one must not lose sight of the fact that being able to identify that risks are being run, and to place a value on those risks, is itself an achievement.

ASSET-VOLATILITY-BASED APPROACHES VERSUS EARNINGS-VOLATILITY-BASED APPROACHES

There is really no correct answer as to which of the two approaches is the better one. The earnings-volatility approach has the advantage that it is very top-down, and provides a link between the risk capital of the individual businesses and the riskiness which the shareholder perceives (volatile earnings). However, it is increasingly difficult to break this down to lower levels of detail, and it cannot be used in pricing an individual transaction, for instance. The asset-volatility approach, on the other hand, suffers from the opposite weakness: it is very good at assessing ex-ante the potential variability in outcomes at low levels of detail, even to price a transaction, but the increasing reliance on unstable correlations makes the tool less and less useful the higher one moves up the consolidation tree.

The best approach is probably a synthesis of the two approaches: earnings volatility can be used as a generic tool to allocate the overall risk capital of the bank down one or two layers in the organisation structure, such as to the individual business. Each individual business will then need to look at the riskiness implied by the earnings-volatility model, and then work out what it is that drives this volatility. These volatility drivers can be modelled—to the extent possible—similar to the way in which credit and market risks were modelled in Chapter 4. An element of residual volatility may have to be accepted as an uncontrollable cost of being in a particular business. Figure 6.3 illustrates how revenue volatility over a period might be explained in terms of market and credit risk (both steerable through an asset-volatility approach), and a residual risk component which cannot be actively controlled.

The recommendation to banks who wish to build an internal asset-volatility RAPM is to combine this at least with a measure of earnings volatility. The latter is relatively easy to assess, and enables management to monitor how closely the asset-volatility approach models the actual earnings volatility experienced—if the model does not reliably and accurately explain nearly all of the earnings volatility, then it is flawed: either the parameters need adjusting or the design of the model itself is faulty. The issue of calibration is one of several practical issues related to measuring risk capital which form the subject of the next chapter.

STATISTICAL APPENDIX: NON-NORMAL EARNINGS DISTRIBUTIONS

This book is not meant to be a treatise on statistics, and it is strongly recommended that, when doing this kind of analysis, sufficient statistical expertise is on hand to assist. However, there are certain features of earnings distributions which even the non-statistician should be aware of, and

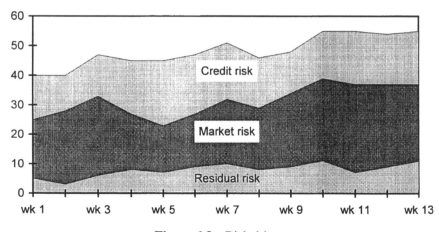

Figure 6.3 Risk drivers

some modifications to the simple normal-distribution model shown in this chapter. The statistical phenomena mentioned here are relevant for any model which uses statistical techniques, including the asset-volatility-based models.

Most earnings distributions are, in practice, non-normal. They tend to exhibit two tendencies: skewness and so-called 'fat tails'.

Skewness is a well-understood statistical concept, and there is even a formula (Pearson's coefficient of skewness) which can be used to measure the extent of this skewness. Figure 6.2 showed the revenue distribution of Theobank, which was clearly negatively skewed—the bars tail off more gradually to the left than to the right. In a normal distribution, the mean, the mode (the most frequently occurring data point) and the median (the mid-point between the highest and lowest values) all occur at the same point—at the peak of the distribution. In a negatively-skewed distribution, the mean is actually somewhere to the left of the peak. This means that the normal way of measuring the standard deviation (taking the difference between the mean and each observation, squaring this, and then taking the square root of the average of these squared amounts) can mis-state the true riskiness of the earnings stream. Both of the alternative deviation measures shown below (modified deviation and objective deviation) go some way to compensating for this lack of normality, as they only regard one side of the distribution (i.e. the lack of symmetry is not relevant). More sophisticated mathematical techniques for dealing with this problem are beyond the scope of this book.

The other non-normal feature of earnings distributions is the phenomenon of 'fat tails'. Despite what the name implies, this has very little to do with the hind quarters of overweight people—it actually refers to distributions where the probability of occurrences at the extreme ends is actually much higher than any statistical model would predict. An example of a fat-tailed distribution is given in Figure 6.4.

This distribution (taken from the daily revenues of a trading portfolio) is a classic example of fat tails. The frequency of daily revenues tails off towards the extremes, as one would expect, and then suddenly re-merges at both extremes with relatively high frequencies. In plain English, one does not often lose much money, but when one does, one loses a lot. It has over the last few years become gradually recognised that virtually all financial markets behave in this way, which has played havoc with many of the assumptions behind risk models in trading rooms.

Whilst statistics has a standard way of dealing with distributions which are more or less peaked than the normal distribution would imply

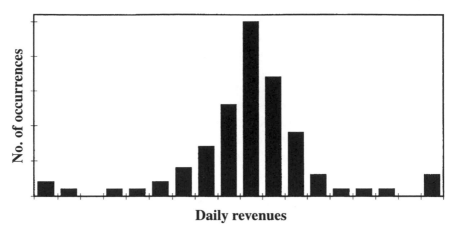

Figure 6.4   Example of a 'fat-tailed' distribution

(this is called kurtosis), there is no mathematical adjustment which can properly deal the problem of fat tails, as statistical models all assume that the relative frequency of occurrences tails off towards the extremes more or less smoothly (even if not symmetrically on both sides).

Altering the confidence interval to a one-tailed test

The first step in adjusting the standard-deviation based model shown in this chapter is to switch to a one-tailed test. The confidence intervals shown in earlier chapters were based on a two-tailed test; that is to say, they looked at the probability of occurrences either side of the mean. This is shown graphically in Figure 6.5.

Here, the probability of being outside two standard deviations (in either direction) is twice 47.73%, or 95.46% in total.

In practice, management is probably only interested in the left-hand side of the distribution (the probability of making less than expected). This can be accommodated by taking a one-sided test, i.e. taking only the probability of being below a certain level, as illustrated in Figure 6.6.

In a one-tailed test, the probability of being below two standard deviations is 50% + 47.73%, or 97.73% in total (the cumulative probability of each side of the distribution is by definition 50%).

It is also easier to work in terms of rounded probabilities rather than a round number of standard deviations—management finds '95% probable' much more intuitive than 'two standard deviations' (or a spuriously precise 97.73% probability). Table 6.8 converts round probabilities into

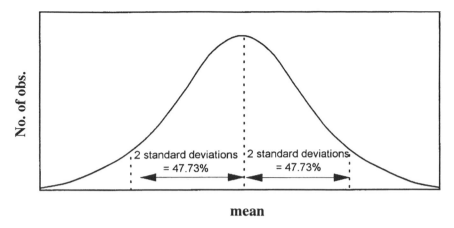

mean

Figure 6.5 Normal distribution: 2-tailed test

standard deviations for a one-sided test. Since the calculation of the standard deviation itself always gives the value for exactly one standard deviation, it is a minor matter to multiply this by the factors in the right-hand column.

Using the modified deviation

The normal method of deriving the standard deviation utilises all observed values, whether above or below the mean. As noted above, distributions are in practice not always symmetrical and, particularly since management are much more concerned with the downside risk rather than the upside, this can significantly distort the actual amount of risk being taken.

Table 6.8 Confidence intervals (one-sided test)

Probability	Number of std. deviations
90.0%	1.28
95.0%	1.64
97.5%	1.96
99.0%	2.33
99.5%	2.57
99.9%	3.08

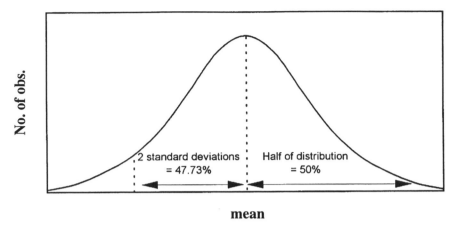

Figure 6.6   Normal distribution: 1-tailed test

A simple way to adjust for this is to take only the negative variances when calculating the deviation. Observations which exceed the mean are ignored. Table 6.9 shows the calculation of both the standard deviation and the modified deviation for Theobank Inc.

(Note that both deviations are calculated by dividing the sum of the variances by one less than the number of observations—23 in the case of the standard deviation and 10 in the case of the modified duration—as we are dealing with a sample and not a full population).

Using the objective deviation

Another measure which focuses on the downside risks only is the objective duration. This measure has been developed by financial analysts[3] to measure the risk of not meeting a given target. For example, a fund manager who is under pressure to meet a certain target might be misled by traditional measures of riskiness, such as the relationship between the mean and the standard deviation.[4] An investment with an expected return of 8%, and with a standard deviation of 2%, might look more attractive than one with an expected return of 12% and a standard deviation of 12%. However, if the fund manager needs to obtain a return of 12%, the first low-risk investment is virtually useless, as there is very little chance of making that return. In the second case, there is at least a 50% chance.

The objective deviation is similar to the modified duration, but it replaces the mean of the sample with the *targeted* mean. In order to focus only on downside risk, it also treats all positive variances as zero.

Table 6.9 Calculation of standard and modified deviations
(Theobank's revenues)

Month	X	Variance	Modified variance
1	237	289	—
2	240	400	—
3	162	3364	3364
4	195	625	625
5	204	256	256
6	190	900	900
7	216	16	16
8	208	144	144
9	213	49	49
10	249	841	—
11	243	529	—
12	182	1444	1444
13	184	1296	1296
14	209	121	121
15	237	289	—
16	225	25	—
17	223	9	—
18	228	64	—
19	245	625	—
20	235	225	—
21	256	1296	—
22	256	1296	—
23	200	400	400
24	243	529	—
Average	220		
Standard Deviation		25.56	
Modified Deviation			29.35

The resulting measure is an extremely useful way of looking at the likelihood that given targets (such as the bank's revenue target) are not going to be met. Businesses with low targets but a high degree of certainty of being achieved might be more interesting than businesses with a potentially high upside, but very high risk, particularly where the bank is very keen to maintain a certain level of earnings (for example, because it needs to raise its capital level, or because it must at least maintain sufficient earnings to pay the dividend). Using the revenues of Theobank, Table 6.10 demonstrates the calculation of the objective deviation.

Table 6.10   Calculation of objective deviation where
objective 240

Month	X	Variance	Objective variance
1	237	289	9
2	240	400	0
3	162	3364	6084
4	195	625	2025
5	204	256	1296
6	190	900	2500
7	216	16	576
8	208	144	1024
9	213	49	729
10	249	841	0
11	243	529	0
12	182	1444	3364
13	184	1296	3136
14	209	121	961
15	237	289	9
16	225	25	225
17	223	9	289
18	228	64	144
19	245	625	0
20	235	225	25
21	256	1296	0
22	256	1296	0
23	200	400	1600
24	243	529	0
Average	220		
Standard Deviation		25.56	
Modified Deviation			32.30

Note that, where the modified duration used only the variances where the value observed was below the mean, for the objective duration all observations are included, but that those which exceed the objective are set equal to zero.

Objective deviation could be used as a measure of risk capital in its own right; at SBC, we use it periodically to test the feasibility of planned revenue targets against historical revenues, and to provide some input when comparing budgets across different businesses.

Using the standard error

A further problem which occurs when we derive a distribution from a historical time series is the fact that the mean itself moves over time (hopefully upwards!). In other words, $100 million of revenue at the beginning of the period may not have the same meaning as $100 million at the end of the period. Figure 6.7 illustrates this graphically, using Theobank's private investor business as an example (see time series in Table 6.3).

The trend line (dotted) shows clearly that the trend is rising upwards. The standard deviation is calculated based on the mean: for example, in the oldest month on the chart ($t-24$), the variance between the mean (100) and the actual value (95) would be used. If we were to use a moving average (the trend line), we would only calculate the difference between the trended average (about 97 at $t-24$) and the observed value. With a marked trend such as in this case, the effect of using a constant mean is to overstate the variance at both the beginning and the end of the series, overstating the standard deviation overall. This is less acute in relatively stable businesses, but can be particularly dangerous in high-growth situations such as new business start-ups.

There is a statistical technique for dealing with this: it is called the *standard error*. This replaces a constant mean with a linear regression and then calculates for each data point the difference between the observed value and the regression line. Mathematically, this is expressed as:

$$SEE = \sqrt{\frac{\sum_{i=1}^{n} e_i^2}{n-2}}$$

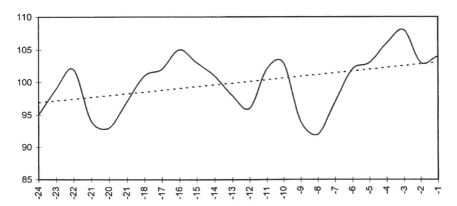

Figure 6.7 Theobank Inc: revenues from private investors

where e^2_i represents the square of the difference between the regression line and the observed value. Note that the denominator is $n-2$ here: we lost one degree of freedom through the fact that we are using a sample, not the whole population, and we lost another through using an assumed trend line through the data. The standard error for the private investor business is \$4.05 million, versus a standard deviation of \$4.39 million.

ENDNOTES

1. Using $(n-1)$ to calculate the variance and standard deviation, as the returns shown are a sample, not the full population.
2. Robert C. Merton and André F. Perold, 'Management of risk capital in financial firms', in *Financial Services: Perspectives and Challenges,* ed. Samuel L. Hayes, Harvard Business School Press, 1993.
3. Neil Wolfson, 'Objective Deviation: An individualised measure of risk', *Journal of Investing,* Spring 1994.
4. The usual method is to apply the Sharpe ratio:

$$\frac{\overline{X} - R_f}{\sigma}$$

or the excess of the expected return over the risk-free rate, divided by the standard deviation of returns.

PART THREE
Limitations of the RoC Approach

7
Feeding the Model: the Importance of Clean Data

Many, if not all, of the models which have been described in this book are either directly derived from the internal management accounts (requiring a stream of revenues, contributions etc. over a series of periods from which to calculate the volatility) or require management accounting numbers (such as 'return') in order to derive an RoC measure. This chapter is dedicated to three technical issues which are likely to be encountered when building these management accounts: differences between mark-to-market and accruals accounting, funds transfer pricing, and expected losses. A particular trap which can be encountered when using a net-present-value accounting approach in conjunction with an RoC model is also examined.

Cost allocation is also an issue in management accounts, but whilst this may affect the definition of 'return' in any RoC, RAROC or RORAC calculation, it is unlikely to have any significant impact on the definition of 'capital' or the measurement of risk, as costs are typically not very volatile in the short term. The topic of appropriate cost allocation techniques is therefore left to other text books: the focus here is on the attribution of revenue to particular periods and to individual businesses. It is emphasised that without a robust method for attributing revenues to businesses it is probably not worthwhile attempting to build any capital allocation model at all; indeed, building a decent series of management accounts is the necessary precursor to any capital allocation process. Firstly, this is because there is not much point allocating capital unless we know what we are allocating it to, and are able to measure how well that capital has been utilised. Secondly, the revenue stream itself may form part of the definition of the capital (earnings-volatility approach). And finally, the risk capital model will need to be 'calibrated': the ex-ante assessment of risk which the model calculated compared to the actual risk taken over the measurement period—this is especially impor-tant in the asset-volatility based models seen in Chapter 4.

MARK-TO-MARKET VERSUS ACCRUALS ACCOUNTING

In '*mark-to-market*' accounting, the definition of revenue for any one period is the change in the market value of the instrument or portfolio over the period, plus/minus any cash flows during the period. It is the method generally used for the trading book. For example, assume a hold-ing of 20 IBM stocks worth $90 at time 0; between that point and time 1, 10 of those stocks are sold for $92, and an additional 10 GM stocks are sold for $50 (i.e. sold short). At time 1, the IBM stocks have a market price of $95 and those of GM $52. Table 7.1 shows the profit for the period on a mark-to-market basis.

The mark-to-market method, therefore, implicitly assumes that the position can be liquidated at the end of each period; the decision not to liquidate is treated as an opportunity cost: it is the same as if the position were liquidated and then re-established. Most banks adjust the calcula-tion slightly, to reflect the fact that it may not be quite so easy to close

Table 7.1   Example of mark-to-market calculation

Value of portfolio at time t_0:		
	Long 20 IBM stocks @ $90	1800
Sell 10 IBM stocks		
	10 stocks @ 92	−920
Sell 10 GM stocks		
	10 stocks @ 50	−500
Balance on portfolio at time t_1		380
Value of portfolio at time t_1		
	Long 10 IBM @ 95	950
	Short 10 GM @ 52	−520
		430
Profit for the period t_0–t_1		
	430 – 380	50

out the position—sometimes, banks take the market bid price as the value for a long position, and the market offer price for short positions (effectively assuming that the bank is on the 'wrong' side of the market each time). Other banks may take the mid-market price, but adjust this with a liquidity factor, which may vary with the size of the position (the larger the position in relationship to the size of the market, the more difficult it becomes to liquidate a position at prevailing prices); this may even result in long positions being marked below the bid and short positions above the offer, to take account of the likely change in market prices if a sufficiently large portfolio were liquidated in a very short space of time.

The similarity between this approach and the 'value-at-risk' concept seen in Chapter 4 should be immediately apparent: whilst VAR attempts to predict what the likely change in market value might be, mark-to-market accounting subsequently measures the actual change in value. Both methods rely on the portfolio being valued at current market prices.

The mark-to-market method is also expanded to cover products for which there is no observable market price (such as some over-the-counter options and other derivatives, which may be unique in terms of strike prices, maturities etc.). Such products can usually be valued by means of a model, which derives the value of the instrument from the potential values of various observable underlying instruments (hence the name 'derivatives'). In such cases, one cannot strictly call the approach 'mark-to-market', as there is no market, and 'net present value' or 'modelled value' might be more appropriate terms. The terms net-present-value (NPV) and mark-to-market (MTM) are used interchangeably in the rest of this chapter.

The *accruals* method is usually applied to the traditional banking activities (loans, deposits etc.), often referred to as the 'banking book' to distinguish it from the trading book. In the accruals method, expected earnings are spread over the life of the product, as is shown in the simple example in Table 7.2.

Whilst it is customary for a bank to use the accruals method for its banking book, it is perfectly possible to value these activities on an NPV basis: the earnings for any given period are calculated as the change in NPV plus/minus any cash inflow/outflow over the period. Table 7.3 shows how the loan example given in Table 7.2 would be accounted for on an NPV basis.

Note that the principal amount of the loan is ignored (it is assumed that this is wholly refinanced in the market). The total earnings over the

Table 7.2   Example of accruals calculation

5-year loan	
Notional amount	$1000
Interest rate	10%
Refinanced at	8%
Annual margin (%)	2%
Annual margin ($)	$20
Earnings per quarter	$5

five-year period ($100) are the same in both cases, but the NPV calculation recognises a significant portion of this at the outset.

The arguments in support of the accruals method are based on the fact that the positions held in the banking book are usually held until maturity; this contrasts with the trading book, where the assumption is that the position could be closed out at any time. Recognising the income over the life of the transaction more fairly matches the costs which are incurred in support of that income stream.

The distinction between the two is, however, becoming more and more blurred: a swap, usually treated as part of the trading book, is also usually held until maturity, whereas many traditional banking products (mortgage loans, credit card receivables) are now commonly repackaged and sold off long before they reach maturity.

The arguments brought in favour of accruals accounting are precisely that: accounting arguments, which have got very little to do with risk. For example, the credit risk profile of a mortgage can look very similar to that of a swap, as was demonstrated earlier. Only mark-to-market accounting can really give the full picture about risks, as it recognises in any one period the full change in value incurred during that period. For

Table 7.3   Loan accounted for under NPV method (Discount rate 10%)

	Year 1	Year 2	Year 3	Year 4	Year 5
Total cash flow	20.0	20.0	20.0	20.0	20.0
PV of remaining cash flow	63.4	49.7	34.7	18.2	0.0
Calculation of earnings:					
Change in PV over period	63.4	−13.7	−15.0	−16.5	−18.2
+Cash inflow	20.0	20.0	20.0	20.0	20.0
=Earnings for period	83.4	6.3	5.0	3.5	1.8

this reason, internal measurements of performance should be performed on an MTM basis if at all possible.

The problem with the banking book is that it is not that easy to apply MTM or NPV accounting. There are a number of reasons for this:

1. Volume of calculations: the sheer number of open transactions on a bank's books at any one point in time is daunting, and they may be spread over a large number of branches and subsidiaries, many of which may be running on different accounting packages.
2. Uncertainty as to timing of cash flows: theoretically, all customers could withdraw their sight deposits tomorrow, but the bank can usually rely on a suitable pool of sight deposits over time (the legal maturity of the individual balances is very different from the economic maturity of the portfolio).
3. Uncertainty as to size of cash flows: many retail banking products (especially mortgages in continental Europe) are not tied to a clear interest rate which enables the bank to lock in the margin (e.g. LIBOR + x), but are repriced periodically based on market and even political pressures.

This complexity has made many banks wary of making the massive investment required to build systems which allow them to determine the NPV of the banking book. However, there are two techniques which at least enable the risks of the banking book to be accounted for when they are incurred, even if the accruals method of accounting is used. These two techniques are:

1. Charge anticipated loan losses against the loan book, based on a statistical loan loss concept similar to the assessment of credit risk seen in Chapter 4. This ensures that changes in the quality of the portfolio are recognised immediately, not deferred until an actual default occurs and specific provisions are made.
2. Funds transfer pricing at market rates. This forces each banking transaction to be refinanced (or invested, if on the liability side) at the appropriate market interest rate matching the maturity of the transaction; the result is to transfer the interest rate risk across to the trading book, where it will be managed on an MTM/NPV basis.

Each of these techniques is examined in turn below.

STATISTICAL LOAN LOSS RESERVES

Accounting for statistically expected loan losses seems like common sense, but is not broadly accepted in the banking industry. After all, life insurance companies regularly make actuarial assessments of the mortality rates of their insured clientele and ensure that their reserves are sufficient to meet this. Martin Taylor, CEO of Barclays Bank, has announced that the bank is trying to introduce such a concept for credit risks, and other banks have also developed similar internal models (SBC introduced the concept in 1992 for the trading businesses and expanded this in 1994 to cover all of the bank). The technique has recently been labelled 'dynamic provisioning', and a debate has started as to whether such provisions should be covered by accounting standards. Banks have so far been reluctant to book any provisions for statistically expected loan losses to the balance sheet of the bank, as this would have the effect of decreasing capital without any offsetting reduction in the regulatory capital requirements (one solution would be for the regulators to allow statistical loan loss provisions to count towards capital, or alternatively the regulatory capital requirements for credit exposures could themselves be reduced in the case of banks which build such statistical reserves).

The basic approach to deriving statistical credit reserves is to break the credit exposures into a matrix by rating and maturity, and then multiply each cell in the matrix by the appropriate statistically expected default rate (see Figure 7.1).

The sum of the cells in the 'expected loan loss' matrix is equivalent to the statistically expected loss over the remaining life of the portfolio. Each business is charged with a risk premium which is based on the statistically expected loss for its credit portfolio, and the amount of the premium credited to a central loan loss reserve. Actual loan losses are then absorbed against the reserve. The businesses are thus forced to account for the risk premium on each credit up front (without this, the businesses report high interest earnings, with periodic loan loss charge-offs which

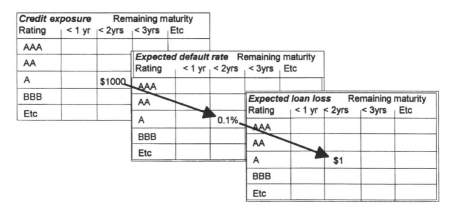

Figure 7.1   Typical statistical expected loan loss model

may be recognised only several years later). Any downgrading in the quality of the portfolio increases the expected default cost, and this cost is charged immediately to the relevant business – this is similar to the mark-to-market approach, in that the credit quality of the portfolio is periodically 'revalued' and the difference taken to P&L.

In addition to the usual problems of getting the basic data and selling the idea to line managers, a number of methodological issues need to be addressed before the system can be implemented.

Where to get default rates from?

Banks which use their own rating systems will need a history of defaults by tenor and rating to build the default cost matrix. Very few banks have invested in the necessary data gathering in the past, and many have over-hauled their rating systems such that the historical rates are not compara-ble with the current system. Public sources of default rates are Moody's,[1] as well as academic analyses of the premium over risk-free rates com-manded by corporate bonds.[2]

How to define credit exposure?

Internal models will need to be established to determine the credit expo-sure linked to contingent credits (such as committed credit lines not yet drawn down) as well as the volatile nature of the credit exposure of derivatives contracts, perhaps using the techniques shown in the previous chapter. At their simplest, these can be covered by crude conversion fac-tors such as those used in regulatory capital requirements. Sophisticated methods include using option valuation models (a contingent credit is, after all, an option to borrow money).

Dealing with collateral and recovery rates

A further problem is the issue of collateral: a loan covered by some por-tion of collateral is clearly likely to result in a lower loss than an unse-cured loan. Getting information on the extent of collateral available (there are myriad forms of collateral available, made even more compli-cated by contracts with trigger provisions, whereby a certain amount of collateral must be posted if certain events occur) is one part of this prob-lem; another is the valuation of whatever collateral is currently held. Again, solutions range from the crude (e.g. assume all mortgages are covered by 80% realisable collateral) to the very sophisticated.

Another facet of the same problem is the issue of recovery rates: even in the case of an unsecured loan, the actual loss incurred is likely to be lower than the default rates suggest, as it is unusual for creditors to lose everything in a liquidation. As with the other issues raised, one can adopt solutions which range from broad assumptions to models which reflect the seniority of the debt, the credit product involved, different experience with different customer classes, the bank's share of the customer's total indebtedness etc.

As with other statistical techniques, it is easy to reach a point where the search for greater mathematical precision goes beyond what is sensible in terms of both the cost involved and the spurious feeling of accuracy which a very sophisticated model may impart. Whatever the level of sophistication involved, the basic steps involved in converting to blank loan equivalent are shown in Figure 7.2.

A final hurdle to be overcome is the 'lumpiness' of the actual default experience—loan losses are not incurred smoothly over time, but fluctuate with such factors as the economic cycle. As loan losses are intended to be charged against the central statistical reserve, this will build up during economic growth periods and deplete as loan loss experience increases during a recession. If the businesses are routinely charged/credited with any shortfall/surplus in the statistical reserve, this will obviate the whole purpose of the reserve. Some sort of cyclical mechanism, such as a time delay, needs to be built into to the system to ensure that 'surplus' reserves are not passed back to the business prematurely.

FUNDS TRANSFER PRICING

The second of the two adjustments to accruals-based performance measurement is a funds transfer pricing system between the central treasury and the banking book, with a view to eliminating the sensitivity to interest rate changes which only mark-to-market accounting can properly reflect.

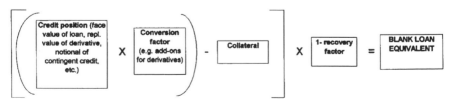

Figure 7.2   Steps involved in converting to a blank loan equivalent

In the earlier loan example (Tables 7.2 and 7.3), it was assumed that both the customer interest rate and the refinancing rate were fixed at the outset, giving a highly predictable margin over the life of the loan. However, banks take advantage of the fact that the yield curve is not flat—usually, it is upwards sloping, and banks will typically fund long-term assets out of short-term liabilities (the liabilities do not have to be shorter in tenor than the assets, just repriced more frequently; typically these are customer deposits which can be theoretically withdrawn at very short notice, but which in practice form a reliable long-term source of funding).

Table 7.4 repeats the example given in Table 7.3 (NPV accounting for a loan), but this time assuming that the refinancing rate changes from 8% to 11% at the end of year 3. On an accruals basis, positive earnings ($20 per year) are shown for the first three years, followed by two years of negative earnings (–$10 per year), giving a total of $40 over the five years. The NPV method also sums to $40 over the five years, but note how the NPV calculation of earnings immediately reflects the change in value of the position in year 3.

This sensitivity to changes in interest rates can be eliminated by requiring all banking book transactions to be refinanced (reinvested in the case of liabilities) with the central treasury at the same duration. If this transfer is done at market rates or a similar opportunity cost of funds, then the banking book is effectively able to lock in the customer margin over the life of the transaction. The central treasury, which is usually measured on an NPV basis, can then decide whether to maintain the

Table 7.4   Change in value caused by change in refinancing rate
(discount rate 10%)

	Year 1	Year 2	Year 3	Year 4	Year 5
Actual cash flows	20.0	20.0	20.0	–10.0	–10.0
= earnings on an accruals basis					
Calculation of earnings on NPV basis:					
Assumed cash flows at t_0	20.0	20.0	20.0	20.0	20.0
Assumed cash flows at t_3				–10.0	–10.0
PV of remaining cash flows	63.4	49.7	34.7	–9.1	0.0
Change in PV over period	63.4	–13.7	–15.0	–43.8	9.1
+ Cash inflow/outflow	20.0	20.0	20.0	–10.0	–10.0
= Earnings for period	83.4	6.3	5.0	–53.8	–0.9

interest risk position which it has acquired, or to amend the risk profile by entering into additional transactions in the market.

If, in the above example, the bank had financed the loan out of client deposits with a six-month maturity, a market-rate funds transfer pricing system would assume that the business responsible for client deposits effectively invested these at the six-month rate, and the business making the loan effectively borrowed from the treasury at the five-year rate, as illustrated in Figure 7.3 (the market rates for six-month and five-year funds are assumed to be 8.5% and 9.5%, respectively—these are only for the purposes of illustration; in practice, the difference between the market and customer rates may be much larger). Note that this transfer of the interest rate risk to the treasury book can apply even if both the loan and the deposit are within the same business or department (this is the approach taken at SBC, where no interest rate risk is allowed to be run outside of the treasury, requiring that every transaction is effectively refinanced/invested with the treasury at the opportunity cost of funds appropriate for its duration).

When the short-term liabilities come to be re-priced in year 3, and the rate has increased to 11%, the businesses continue to enjoy a locked-in interest rate: the loan is still refinanced internally at 9.5% and the deposits continue to earn a spread of 50 basis points (internal rate 11.5%). The result is that the treasury takes a loss of 200 basis points, as shown in Figure 7.4, unless it has otherwise hedged its yield curve exposure. The total margin for the bank is a negative 100 basis points (10%

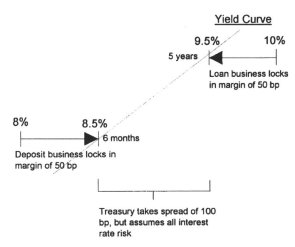

Figure 7.3 Funds transfer pricing between treasury and other businesses

–11%), as before, but the businesses show a positive margin of 100 basis points whilst the treasury shows a loss of 200 basis points.

An accounting problem can arise under this method, however—if the treasury is measured on an NPV basis and the banking book on an accruals basis, the opposite sides of the funds transfer between the two will be valued differently, giving rise to a profit or loss for any particular period which is not automatically eliminated on consolidation. This difference—which will tend to zero over time, as it is only a timing difference—needs to be reconciled regularly and eliminated on consolidation to avoid over- or under-stating profits for a given period.

THE NPV TRAP—ACCOUNTING FOR THE FUTURE COST OF CAPITAL

The NPV basis of accounting can lead to a dangerous mis-statement of true performance when combined with a return-on-capital type of measure, unless great care is taken to avoid the potential pitfalls.

For example, the loan officer in the above example is able to make a loan with a fixed rate of 10% over 5 years (assume that the 10% is net of any deduction for statistically-expected credit losses), and is able to lock in funding at 9.5% over the same period (perhaps even is forced to do under the funds transfer pricing model), and he has therefore effectively guaranteed a margin of 0.5% over five years. The NPV approach would recognise this, and credit his P&L account with the full value—not quite

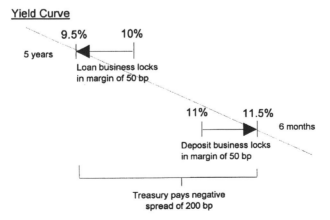

Figure 7.4 Funds transfer pricing: short-term rates move to 11%

2.5%, as the cash flows in future periods have to be discounted, but certainly not the 0.5% per annum which traditional accruals-based accounting recognises.

There is, however, one fundamental difference between mark-to-market accounting and NPV accounting: the mark-to-market approach operates under the assumption of a liquid market i.e. that positions could be liquidated at the time of valuation, at a price at least close to the market price (large positions which could not be unloaded without impacting the market should be valued conservatively, by deducting a 'liquidity allowance'). This same assumption does not necessarily hold true for a swap or a loan, which may have to be held until maturity.

Thus in the example of a loan measured on an NPV basis, it is important to remember that the loan also locks in *capital* for the duration. This is crucial when measuring performance based on return on capital, as the 'capital' in the denominator is usually based on the capital locked in at a point in time.

Conceptually, the RoC equation reads:

$$\frac{\text{multi-period return (discounted)}}{\text{single-period return}}$$

It does not matter here whether 'capital' is regulatory capital, risk capital or some other measure: as long as the capital measure does not take into account the tenor of the transaction, the result will be an incentive to maximise apparent RoC by doing longer and longer deals. A simple example will illustrate the point: assume that the loan used in the earlier example was in the amount of $1000, that interest payments take place at the end of each year, and that the loan is match-funded with a margin of 2% (these assumptions are not critical—they just make the example easier to follow). Assume also that the capital requirement is $100 (giving a somewhat unrealistic RoC of 20% p.a. under accruals accounting, but it will help to illustrate the point). Table 7.5 shows the resulting RoC calculation under NPV accounting and using a cost of capital of 10% to discount the cash flows.

(As previously noted, it is not necessary to discount the exchange of principal at the outset and on maturity, as the assumption of match-funding matches all cash-flows, leaving only the incremental margin).

Note that the sum of the revenues recorded in the 'Earnings for period' line add up to the actual margin earned ($100) over the period, but that there is a very significant 'front loading' of the revenue, and hence also of the RoC, with the result that the return earned in future

Table 7.5   RoC under NPV method (discount rate 10%)

	Year 1	Year 2	Year 3	Year 4	Year 5
Margin	20.0	20.0	20.0	20.0	20.0
PV of remaining cash flows	63.4	49.7	34.7	18.2	0.0
Change in NPV	63.4	−13.7	−15.0	−16.5	−18.2
Cash inflow	20.0	20.0	20.0	20.0	20.0
Earnings for period	83.4	6.3	5.0	3.5	1.8
Capital	100	100	100	100	100
RoC (%)	**83.4**	**6.3**	**5.0**	**3.5**	**1.8**

years does not come close to covering the cost of the capital tied in. To see how badly this distorts the picture, consider the same loan over a ten-year period (Table 7.6).

The loan officer could almost double his RoC in the first year just by doing a ten year loan for the same terms! Of course, he has generated a larger positive cash flow for the bank, and hence deserves some reward, but the simple RoC equation does not consider the fact that he has also locked in capital for double the period. Many banks learned this lesson in the early 1990s the hard way, as the swaps market grew not only in size but also in complexity and tenor of the transactions, with swaps over 10 years becoming not uncommon. Traders were often rewarded on the basis of their return on capital, with the result that they earned huge bonuses, and left banks with medium- to long-term portfolios that barely covered the cost of the capital tied up in them. The argument that such

Table 7.6   RoC under NPV method—10 year example (discount rate 10%)

	Year 1	Year 2	Year 3	Year 4	Year 5	Year 6	Year 7	Year 8	Year 9	Year 10
Margin	20.0	20.0	20.0	20.0	20.0	20.0	20.0	20.0	20.0	20.0
PV of remaining cash flows	115.2	106.7	97.4	87.1	75.8	63.4	49.7	34.7	18.2	0.0
Change in NPV	115.2	−8.5	−9.3	−10.3	−11.3	−12.4	−13.7	−15.0	−16.5	−18.2
Cash inflow	20.0	20.0	20.0	20.0	20.0	20.0	20.0	20.0	20.0	20.0
Earnings for period	135.2	11.5	10.7	9.7	8.7	7.6	6.3	5.0	3.5	1.8
Capital	100	100	100	100	100	100	100	100	100	100
RoC (%)	**135.2**	**11.5**	**10.7**	**9.7**	**8.7**	**7.6**	**6.3**	**5.0**	**3.5**	**1.8**

portfolios could be sold, thus releasing the capital, is disingenuous, as any buyer (if one could be found) would wish to negotiate a sufficient discount so as to cover the cost of *his* capital tied up.

Table 7.7 shows what happens. It is based on a growing portfolio of transactions (for example, swaps or loans), each one hedged against interest rate risk and locking in a margin of $20 per year for five years. Each year, a new transaction is added (so that after the fifth year, the portfolio stabilises with a new transaction being written to replace each maturing one). The calculation of the earnings is not repeated, as this is the same as before.

The RoC is, as in the earlier example (Table 7.5), very high in the first year; in the second year it falls, as the high return on the new transaction is averaged with the return on the first transaction (note that the capital tied up doubles, as there are now two transactions in the portfolio). The RoC continues to fall until the fifth year, and thereafter stabilises as the book remains constant in size, with a new transaction replacing the one which matures each year. Thus the RoC patterns are different from year to year, unless the book is completely stable, and yet the performance—writing a new transaction each year and locking in a fixed margin—is

Table 7.7   Rolling portfolio of credits (discount rate 10%)

	Year 1	Year 2	Year 3	Year 4	Year 5	Year 6
Margin:						
Trans. 1	20	20	20	20	20	
Trans. 2		20	20	20	20	20
Trans. 3			20	20	20	20
Trans. 4				20	20	20
Trans. 5					20	20
Trans. 6						20
Earnings:						
Trans. 1	83.4	6.3	5.0	3.5	1.8	
Trans. 2		83.4	6.3	5.0	3.5	1.8
Trans. 3			83.4	6.3	5.0	3.5
Trans. 4				83.4	6.3	5.0
Trans. 5					83.4	6.3
Trans. 6						83.4
Trans. 7						
Total	**83.4**	**89.7**	**94.7**	**98.2**	**100.0**	**100.0**
Capital	100	200	300	400	500	500
RoC (%)	**83.4**	**44.9**	**31.6**	**24.5**	**20.0**	**20.0**

identical. The salesman who did the transactions in the first years has probably retired to the Bahamas to write his memoirs, whilst the poor chap who joined thereafter to replace him, and who is doing exactly the same job with the same level of success, is going to appear to be performing at a much lower level.

This phenomenon can lead to managers over-paying bonuses during the growing years of a business, and if the business were to turn into a period of decline, one could show that exactly the same phenomenon would lead to managers under-paying bonuses for identical performance whilst the portfolio shrinks in size.

There are at least three different ways of adjusting for this phenomenon.

Use the banks' own cost of capital, not the risk-free rate, to discount revenues

Increasing the discount rate in the NPV calculation from the risk-free to the bank's cost of capital provides only a very partial adjustment—Table 7.8 shows the result if the cost of capital is 15%.

The calculation of earnings is not repeated in detail, as it is the same as in the previous examples, just using a different discount rate. The

Table 7.8   Rolling portfolio of credits (discount rate 15%)

	Year 1	Year 2	Year 3	Year 4	Year 5	Year 6
Margin:						
Trans. 1	20	20	20	20	20	
Trans. 2		20	20	20	20	20
Trans. 3			20	20	20	20
Trans. 4				20	20	20
Trans. 5					20	20
Trans. 6						20
Earnings:						
Trans. 1	77.1	8.6	6.8	4.9	2.6	
Trans. 2		77.1	8.6	6.8	4.9	2.6
Trans. 3			77.1	8.6	6.8	4.9
Trans. 4				77.1	8.6	6.8
Trans. 5					77.1	8.6
Trans. 6						77.1
Trans. 7						
Total	**77.1**	**85.7**	**92.5**	**97.4**	**100.0**	**100.0**
Capital	100	200	300	400	500	500
RoC (%)	**77.1**	**42.8**	**30.8**	**24.3**	**20.0**	**20.0**

difference in RoC is cosmetic only—there is still a substantial front-loading.

Charge the future cost of capital against current period earnings

A more appropriate adjustment is to treat the future cost of capital as a deduction from earnings—after all, if future revenues are to be discounted, then why not future costs as well? This can be done at the risk-free rate, at the cost of capital or some other rate—it does not really matter very much. Table 7.9 shows the result, assuming that the cost of capital is 15%, and using the risk-free rate (10%) as the discount factor.

Table 7.9   Charging the future cost of capital (discount rate 10%)

	Year 1	Year 2	Year 3	Year 4	Year 5	Year 6
Earnings (as before)						
Total	**83.4**	**89.7**	**94.7**	**98.2**	**100.0**	**100.0**
Capital tied up:						
Trans. 1	100	100	100	100	100	
Trans. 2		100	100	100	100	100
Trans. 3			100	100	100	100
Trans. 4				100	100	100
Trans. 5					100	100
Trans. 6						100
Trans. 7						etc.
Cost of future capital:						
Trans. 1		15	15	15	15	
Trans. 2			15	15	15	15
Trans. 3				15	15	15
Trans. 4					15	15
Trans. 5						15
Trans. 6						etc.
Reserve for capital costs:						
Trans. 1	47.5	−10.2	−11.3	−12.4	−13.6	
Trans. 2		47.5	−10.2	−11.3	−12.4	−13.6
Trans. 3			47.5	−10.2	−11.3	−12.4
Trans. 4				47.5	−10.2	−11.3
Trans. 5					47.5	−10.2
Trans. 6						47.5
Total	**47.5**	**37.3**	**26.0**	**13.6**	**0.0**	**0.0**
Adjusted return:	**35.8**	**52.4**	**68.7**	**84.5**	**100.0**	**100.0**
Capital	100	200	300	400	500	500
RoC (%)	**35.8**	**26.2**	**22.9**	**21.1**	**20.0**	**20.0**

Each year a reserve is created, equal to the net present value of the cost of the capital which is tied up in the portfolio for future years at any one point in time. The charge to the portfolio is equal to the change on this reserve—so in the example of transaction 1, there is charge in the first year and then a release of the reserve in future years.

In the first year, the charge is equal to the establishment of the reserve. This is calculated by discounting the future cost of capital, as follows:

$$\frac{\text{year 2 (\$15)}}{(1.10)} + \frac{\text{year 3 (\$15)}}{(1.10)^2} + \frac{\text{year 4 (\$15)}}{(1.10)^3} + \frac{\text{year 5 (\$15)}}{(1.10)^4} = \$47.5$$

In the second year, the required balance on the reserve is:

$$\frac{\text{year 3 (\$15)}}{(1.10)} + \frac{\text{year 4 (\$15)}}{(1.10)^2} + \frac{\text{year 5 (\$15)}}{(1.10)^3} = \$37.3$$

and thus the adjustment to earnings is a release of the reserve in the amount of $10.2. The same calculation is repeated at the end of each year.

Although this may look complicated, in practice it is very easy to calculate, and does not require a separate calculation for each individual transaction (this was shown here for the sake of clarity only). The reserve at any point in time can be calculated by taking the projected capital requirements of the portfolio at that time (assuming no new transactions are to be entered into), charging each year's requirement with the annual cost of capital, and then discounting the result back to the present. The result is that the RoC progression is not as steep as it was previously, although it is still not flat. This is because any return which is in excess of the cost of capital is still recognised up front.

Treat future capital requirements as part of the denominator

The third alternative is similar to discounting the future cost of capital, but instead the capital itself is discounted and then added to the current capital requirement. So whilst the previous alternative adjusted the return (the numerator in the RoC equation) downwards to take full account of the cost of capital, this method adjusts the denominator upwards, as illustrated in Table 7.10.

Again, the *change* in the future capital requirement is used, not the requirement itself; this is added to the current capital requirement. Thus

Table 7.10   Discounting the future capital requirement (discount rate 10%)

	Year 1	Year 2	Year 3	Year 4	Year 5	Year 6
Earnings (as before)						
Total	**83.4**	**89.7**	**94.7**	**98.2**	**100.0**	**100.0**
Capital tied up:						
Trans. 1	100	100	100	100	100	
Trans. 2		100	100	100	100	100
Trans. 3			100	100	100	100
Trans. 4				100	100	100
Trans. 5					100	100
Trans. 6						100
Trans. 7						etc.
NPV of future capital:						
Swap 1	317.0	−68.3	−75.1	−82.6	−90.9	
Swap 2		317.0	−68.3	−75.1	−82.6	−90.9
Swap 3			317.0	−68.3	−75.1	−82.6
Swap 4				317.0	−68.3	−75.1
Swap 5					317.0	−68.3
Swap 6						317.0
Current capital:	100.0	200.0	300.0	400.0	500.0	500.0
Total capital	**417.0**	**448.7**	**473.6**	**490.9**	**500.0**	**500.0**
RoC (%)	**20.0**	**20.0**	**20.0**	**20.0**	**20.0**	**20.0**

for transaction 1, at the outset the addition to capital is equal to the present value of future capital requirements, namely:

$$\frac{\text{year 2 (\$100)}}{(1.10)} + \frac{\text{year 3 (\$100)}}{(1.10)^2} + \frac{\text{year 4 (\$100)}}{(1.10)^3} + \frac{\text{year 5 (\$100)}}{(1.10)^4} = \$317$$

The adjustment to capital for the second year is found firstly by recalculating the required balance on the reserve:

$$\frac{\text{year 3 (\$100)}}{(1.10)} + \frac{\text{year 4 (\$100)}}{(1.10)^2} + \frac{\text{year 5 (\$100)}}{(1.10)^3} = \$248.7$$

and then charging or crediting the difference to the capital balance ($248.7–$317.0 = a credit of $68.3). The result is as close to a smooth series of RoC as one can get.

As with the adjustment to the numerator for the future cost of capital, there is no need to perform the calculation individually for each transaction: the reserve for capital can be calculated for the whole portfolio and the movement on the reserve added or deducted from the current year capital requirement.

The choice of method depends really on management philosophy—method 3 should result in indifference to the tenor of the transactions entered into, whereas method 2 still encourages longer-term engagements which tie up capital for longer. However, method 2 clearly gives recognition now for locking in returns which are greater than the cost of capital, whilst still ensuring that the future return will at least cover the cost of capital. Since both methods use the same information—the future capital requirement—there is no difference between them as to ease of calculation.

IMPORTANCE OF CALIBRATION

A final note in this technical chapter addresses the important but often-overlooked issue of calibration—the process of comparing the output of the model with observed reality, and changing the settings if necessary. All capital allocation and performance measurement models need to be calibrated regularly, to ensure that they reflect the true nature of the business as closely as possible. This is because such models are precisely that: models, or attempts to replicate mathematically the much more complicated processes of the real world. These processes change, and what was previously a reasonable assumption in a model may no longer be appropriate. Calibration is raised here in this technical chapter on management accounts because those management accounts may often be the only yardstick against which the model can be compared, and thus they need to be robust and reliable.

This is especially important when using asset-volatility-based models, which have as their underlying assumption the premise that all material risks can be identified, expressed mathematically and calculated on a regular basis. The only indication as to whether this is really the case is whether the actual volatility of earnings is accurately predicted by the model.

One needs to be careful with the previous statement—this does not mean that at on any one day the value-at-risk model predicts how much money is made or lost. The model parameters might assume that the market moves by 5%, using a 99% confidence interval, but the market might not move at all. This is not inconsistent—the confidence interval simply indicates the probability of the market moving by *no more than* 5%. It is more interesting to review the results of the value-at-risk model over time: if actual losses incurred exceed the values given by the model more than 1% of the time (using a 99% confidence interval), then the model may be wrongly calibrated. This test is easily performed by comparing the time series of actual daily P&L movements with the value-at-risk amounts calculated for each of the same days.

Calibration also involves a less quantifiable task—namely, ensuring that the signals sent out by the model are still consistent with the bank's strategic goals and management philosophy, and that the measurement paradigm is not being arbitraged in some way. For example, a bank might have set out with a problem meeting its regulatory capital requirements, and thus focuses on the optimisation of this constraint. After a period, it may no longer be faced with the same problem, and thus continuing to focus on (unadjusted) regulatory capital could lead to the suboptimal allocation of available capital demonstrated earlier when discussing regulatory capital requirements (Chapter 3). Even if the constraint to be optimised is still valid, it is possible for employees to act in ways which are consistent with the model but not with management's objectives: an example of how a well-meant measure can motivate behaviour designed to improve the performance measure at the expense of the long-term interest of the bank was given in the previous section (future cost of capital).

SUMMARY

It is very important for banks to measure performance (and thus allocate capital) on an economic basis, regardless of whatever financial accounting standards they may be required to obey, as transactions which enhance the value of the organisation need to be rewarded in the period in which they are initiated, not when they are recognised in the books. This usually means adopting a mark-to-market or NPV approach wherever possible, or at least match-funding transactions and deducting expected credit risk costs as a proxy. When measuring performance on an NPV basis, management needs to ensure that all components of the measurement paradigm (e.g. capital as well as returns) are looked at over matching horizons.

This can lead to a management conflict which is difficult, if not impossible, to solve: if employees are rewarded based on an internal, management-accounting-based, measure, then it might be difficult to explain the level of bonuses to shareholders, whose dividends can only be paid out of financial accounting profits, if the latter measure is significantly lower than the internal measure. On the other hand, if the employee who performs well on an NPV basis is not rewarded according to his performance, he will not be motivated to produce business which is economically worth while over the long term, and may leave the bank to join a competitor.

The only possible solution to this conundrum would be for banks to produce their financial accounts on a mark-to-market/NPV basis—but it is far from certain whether their managements (or indeed their shareholders) could stomach the resulting substantial increase in earnings volatility!

ENDNOTES

1. For example *Corporate Bond Defaults and Default Rates 1970–1994*, Moody's Investors Service; New York; January 1995.
2. See Edward Altman, 'Measuring corporate bond mortality and performance', *Journal of Finance*, September 1989.

8
The Limitations of RoC:
the Stock Market's Perspective

Throughout this book, it has been a fundamental assumption that management can improve performance by allocating capital more efficiently, and thus generate a higher return on that capital. This chapter looks at whether the stock market sees it quite the same way. After all, if the shareholders are not benefiting from management's investment of their capital, how can we talk about 'improving performance'? What better benchmark is there for measuring the success of an investment other than the return to the investor?

DIFFERENCE BETWEEN INTERNAL
MEASUREMENT OF RETURN AND THE
SHAREHOLDERS' PERSPECTIVE

A fundamental problem is that the stock market does indeed measure performance on a different basis to the way management (usually) does. The internal measure of return on capital is usually derived by dividing earnings (return) by the available capital. The intention behind RAROC or other RAPM models is to ensure that capital is used efficiently, and thus the return is measured based on *utilisation*; however, the ultimate test of the efficiency of this process must be simply the return generated on the capital *available* for investment. (As in earlier chapters, no distinction is made here between capital and equity for the sake of simplification, but obviously it is just as easy to distinguish between the return on capital and the return on equity, with the latter being the more relevant measure when the returns to shareholders are being considered). The shareholders themselves, however, measure their returns based on the yield derived from owning the stock. Figure 8.1 illustrates the difference between the internal and shareholder view of returns.

A simple example illustrates the difference, and the boundary conditions under which both the internal and shareholder perspectives produce the same result. Imagine two banks, both with $10 billion in capital and expected earnings of $1 billion. The shareholders of bank A require a 10% return on their investment, whereas the investors in bank B require a higher return—say, 15%—to compensate them for the fact that bank B's earnings are more volatile. Both banks are expected to pay all of their earnings out in full as dividends. The implied value of the capital of the two banks is shown in Table 8.1.

Notice how the value of the capital of bank B falls from $10 billion to only $6.7 billion, as the only way for an investor to get a yield of 15% if the expected return is $1 billion is to invest $6.7 billion. The result is that the value of the initial investment falls from $10 billion to $6.7 billion. The relationship between the market value of a bank's equity and the book value is known as the 'price/book ratio' or 'market/book ratio', and is a key indicator of whether a bank is generating returns sufficient to meet the expectation of the investors.

In the case of bank A, the return generated exactly equals the expectations of the investors, and—all other things being equal—the book value of the equity will equal the market value. Under what conditions could one expect this to be true?

The measurement of return in the eyes of the investor involves more than just the actual earnings generated by the bank in a particular period—it involves the expectations of other investors as to the develop-

	Internal Return	Return to Shareholders
Return	Period earnings	Dividends + capital gains
Capital	Book value of capital	Cost of investment

Figure 8.1 Difference between internal return and return to shareholders

Table 8.1 Impact of required returns on value of capital

	Bank A	Bank B
Expected earnings	1000	1000
Required return	10%	15%
Value of capital	10 000	6667

ment of future earnings. This is because the return to the investor is equal to any dividend he receives plus any capital gain on the change in the price of the stock. The price of the stock itself reflects simply the market's assessment of the future dividends which will be paid, discounted at a rate appropriate to the riskiness (uncertainty) of those dividends. Thus, in the case of bank A, if the market reasonably expects dividends to equal $1 billion per year on average and continues to require a 10% return for an investment with this level of risk, then it is reasonable to assume that the value of the bank's equity will remain at $10 billion.

Of course, expectations are constantly changing—expectations as to the level of future dividends, as to the riskiness of those dividends, and as to the level of underlying interest rates (the required return is, under the capital asset pricing model shown in Chapter 5, made up of a risk-free rate plus a risk premium)—and thus the value of stocks fluctuates constantly. However, in general it should hold true that, over time, banks which consistently meet or exceed market expectations will see their stock price rise relative to the stock market in general. One of the methods of managing and measuring this is demonstrated in Chapter 9, which looks at shareholder value and its application in banks.

THE PRICE/BOOK RATIO

This simple ratio (the market value of equity divided by the book value), is a very useful tool when assessing whether banks are generating value for their shareholders, or at least whether shareholders believe that the bank is going to do so.

Table 8.2 shows typical price/book ratios for different types of banks.

It is interesting to note that banks specialising in institutional asset management have much higher price/book ratios than other banks. Why should this be? The reason lies in the fact that this is a relatively new

Table 8.2   Typical price/book ratios

	Median	Mean	High	Low
Universal banks	**1.17**	1.26	1.77	0.88
Investment banks	**0.99**	1.06	1.56	0.47
Global investment banks	**1.07**	1.11	1.28	0.98
Asset mgt—private	**1.99**	2.63	4.49	0.84
Asset mgt—institutional	**5.45**	6.49	10.43	4.91
Retail banks	**1.49**	1.58	2.42	1.17
Overall	**1.42**	2.16		

market with very high growth expectations, with the result that investors are prepared to pay very large premia in the anticipation of future gains. The stock price is very sensitive to investors' future expectations, and the high price/book ratios are due more to these high expectations rather than historically good earnings.

The price/book ratio can be used to adjust the internal RoC targets of the bank. In the earlier example of bank B (Table 8.1), the price/book ratio was only 0.67, as the market value of the capital was only two thirds of the book value. The management of bank B knows that the market is expecting a return of 15%, and if an internal measure of RoC is used, they will conclude that they must earn $1.5 million (15% of $10 billion) in order to meet market demands. However, any return in excess of $1 billion will actually enhance shareholder value, as it will exceed the market's expectations. The price/book ratio can thus be used to calibrate the internal RoC target:

Internal (book value) RoC = Market's expected return × Price/book ratio

In a bank where the price/book ratio is exactly one, such as bank A, the internal RoC benchmark is equal to the market's expected return (the bank's cost of capital). Thus for banks whose stock price has risen such that the price/book ratio is greater than one, setting an RoC hurdle rate which is equal to the cost of capital will actually result in a diminution of value. Imagine a third bank, bank C, again with $10 billion book value, but this time with a price/book ratio of 1.5. If bank C's shareholders require a 10% return, how much must the bank earn?

Using the formula given above, the bank's internal RoC target must be at least equal to:

$$10\% \times 1.5 = 15\%$$

If the management of the bank have failed to understand this point, they might set a target of 12% and conclude that, since this is in excess of the cost of capital, they are creating value. From the shareholder's perspective however, this represents a return of only 8%:

$$\frac{\text{expected earnings}}{\text{market value of equity}} = \frac{\$1200}{\$15\,000} = 8\%$$

and the value of the stock will fall to $12 billion, to ensure that the shareholder gets his required return:

$$\frac{\text{expected earnings}}{\text{required return}} = \text{market value of equity}$$

$$\frac{\$1200}{10\%} = \$12 \text{ billion}$$

The consequence of this is that banks must constantly improve the returns they are earning if they wish to enhance value for shareholders. An already successful bank may have to produce a book (internal) RoC of 20% or more just to maintain value, whilst a less successful bank may be able to enhance value with a book RoC which is actually lower than its cost of capital (if the price/book ratio is less than one).

Failure to understand the difference between the market value and book value of equity can also lead to some very false conclusions about the nature of risk capital. In Chapter 5, a relationship was established between earnings volatility and the cost of capital. Now consider again banks A and B in the earlier example, and assume that the standard deviation of A's earnings is 10% and that of B is 20%. Table 8.3 repeats the regression table produced in the earlier chapter (Table 5.2).

The table suggests that bank A's beta is 1.22; assuming a risk-free rate of 5% and a market premium of 4%, and using the capital asset pricing model, the cost of capital is:

$$k_e = 5\% + (1.22 \times 4\%) = 9.88\%$$

rounded to 10%, as above. Likewise, in the case of bank B, the cost of capital is:

$$k_e = 5\% + (2.30 \times 4\%) = 14.2\%$$

again rounded to 15%, as above.

Table 8.3   Derivation of beta from revenue volatility

Std. dev. of annual revenues as % of average	Modelled beta
4	0.58
6	0.79
8	1.00
10	1.22
12	1.44
14	1.65
16	1.87
18	2.09
20	2.30

Based on the regression, beta = 0.14 + (10.82 × volatility).
The numbers in the table have been rounded slightly.

Now consider the relationship between capital and earnings volatility. In the case of bank A, earnings volatility (one standard deviation) is 10% of the mean i.e. 10% of $1 billion, or $100 million. Thus the capital of bank A is 100 times the earnings volatility (measured as one standard deviation). In the case of bank B, earnings volatility is 20%; given that average earnings are also $1 billion, this means that the standard deviation of the earnings must be $200 million. Capital is thus 50 times the earnings volatility. (Note: in Chapter 5, revenue volatility, not earnings volatility, was used. The distinction is not important here, as the example is illustrative only).

The multiple of capital to the standard deviation of earnings is double in the case of bank A, and yet it is a much less risky bank! How can this be? Surely, since capital exists to absorb risk (probable losses), bank B should actually have more capital than bank A?

This false conclusion derives from the assumption that the stock market can be used to determine what the RoC should be: in fact, the stock market tells us what the cost of capital (probably) is, not what the RoC should be. The difference arises because the stock market's measure of return (change in market value of equity, plus any dividends received, divided by the market value of equity at the beginning of the period) is different to the internal measure of return (earnings for the period divided by the book value of capital). In the case of bank B, the relationship between the volatility of earnings and the market value of its capital actually falls even further, to 33 ($6.7 billion divided by $200 million), as the market devalues the equity based on the fact that returns are not sufficient to compensate for the risk.

RELATIONSHIP BETWEEN PRICE/BOOK RATIO AND RoC

Is there any relationship, then, between price/book ratios and a bank's RoC track record? Figure 8.2 plots price/book ratios against return on equity (remember that for the sake of simplicity the examples used above equate capital with equity) for a sample of 36 banks, covering the range of activities shown in Table 8.2. It is interesting to note that, although there is some relationship between the two ratios, the causality is not as strong as one might have expected.

One might expect that the weakness in the causality lies in the fact that, as noted earlier, price/book ratios of certain banks (asset managers) are more a reflection of future earnings expectations than actual earnings history. However, if we break the regression down into classes (Retail banks, asset managers, etc.), we find that the causality is even lower than when we look at the full sample; Figure 8.3 shows the investment banks, by way of example.

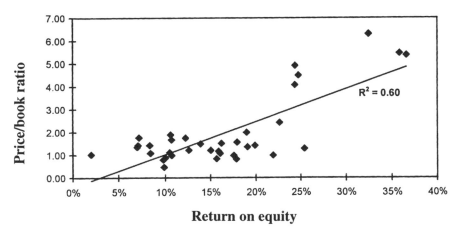

Figure 8.2   Relationship of price/book ratio to RoE

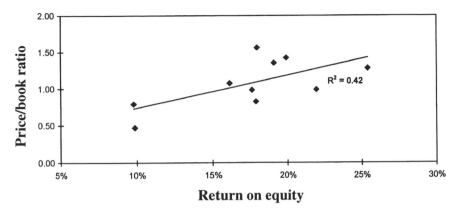

Figure 8.3   Relationship of price/book ratio to RoE: investment banks

The weakness of this causality can be illustrated by two banks which were first encountered in Chapter 1: Lloyds and Bankers Trust. Both of these institutions generated returns on available equity in excess of 20% regularly throughout the last decade—performance which many bank managers would like to emulate. However, as Figure 8.4 shows, Lloyds clearly outperformed its home stock market, whereas Bankers was less successful (relative performance against the home markets is used, as otherwise the two stock prices would have to be adjusted to reflect the different values of the two currencies and the different levels of interest rates over the period).

Despite similar performance in terms of book returns on equity, it would appear that Bankers Trust was unable to match Lloyds in turning this into lasting performance on the stock market. It is not totally clear why this should be, but the most likely explanation is that the market considered that Bankers' business was inherently more risky than its earnings stream suggested, and questioned the ability of the bank to maintain that level of performance. When we consider that Lloyds is primarily in the rather mundane business of retail and commercial banking, whereas Bankers Trust is one of the pioneers of modern financial engineering, it is easy to understand the scepticism of the market. The moral for management must be that it is not sufficient to generate good returns: the market must believe in your ability to continue to do so.

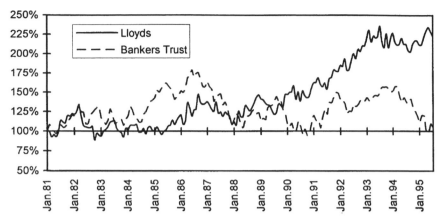

Figure 8.4   Relative stock price performance: Lloyds Bank vs Bankers Trust
Source: Datastream

LIMITATIONS OF USING RoC AS A PERFORMANCE TARGET

The examples shown above show that there is no guaranteed link between a strong internally measured internal RoC and a positive assessment of that performance by the stock market. This is due to two factors: the need to convince the market of the sustainability of earnings and the single-period nature of the RoC metric itself.

The comparison of Bankers Trust with Lloyds highlighted the need to convince the market of the sustainability of earnings, and supports the contention that a good internal RoC does not necessarily mean value for shareholders. However, a glance at the regression analysis (Figure 8.2) does at least indicate that the obverse is true: no bank with a high price/book ratio has a low return on capital. Thus whereas improving RoC is no *guarantee* of success, it would seem on the other hand to be at least a *prerequisite* of success.

The problem with the single-period nature of RoC has at its root the same criticism that has been levelled at Return on Investment (ROI) in a manufacturing setting, and which led to the development of SVA and EVA measures which are the subject of the next chapter: the metric covers only performance over a relatively short period, and does not reflect what management has done to improve future performance. It is even possible to maximise RoC (or ROI) in the short-term at the expense of the firm's future—by suppressing necessary investment, for instance. As the stock market values future earnings potential as well as current earnings, a dichotomy appears between the internal and external measures. Typically, the value of the next dividend payment—the amount influenced by current year earnings—makes up only between 5% and 10% of the total value of the stock. For example, assume that the next dividend is expected to be $10, and that the stock is valued using the dividend growth model, which assumes a growing perpetuity, starting at $10 and growing by 3% per year, viz.:

$$\frac{D}{r-g} = \frac{\$10}{10\% - 3\%} = \$142.8$$

The value of the next dividend payment is only $10, which must be discounted by one year to today's value, i.e. $9.1. This is only 6.3% of the total value of the stock.

Since the value of the bank's stock is much more susceptible to changes in estimates as to the long-term growth potential, it is clear that a focus on current-year RoC alone is of questionable utility.

The lesson from the stock market for managers would therefore appear to be twofold:

1. Beware of relying too blindly on the internal measure of RoC. In addition to the uncertainty as to exactly how much return the shareholders really do expect, the internal RoC model can give very misleading results if the difference between market and book value of equity—the price/book ratio—is ignored.
2. Whereas producing an RoC which is above the cost of capital is a prerequisite of success, it is by no means a guarantee.

The next chapter addresses the problems of the one-year RoC performance metric, introducing a multi-year metric which also takes account of the market's view of required returns.

—— 9 ——

Shareholder Value as a Key
Performance Measure

Back in 1990, the concept of shareholder value creation was not high on the agenda of most bankers; indeed, even as the author pens these lines in the summer of 1995, the concept is still alien to many. However, the topic is gradually increasing in popularity: for example, the 1990 Chief Executive's Report of Lloyds Bank opens under the heading 'Creating shareholder value'. Brian Pitman, the CEO, goes on to write '. . . our objective is to produce for shareholders long-term, superior total returns, comprising progressive dividend growth and appreciation in the share price.' As Chapter 1 showed, Lloyds Bank has certainly achieved that (see *Figure 9.1*).

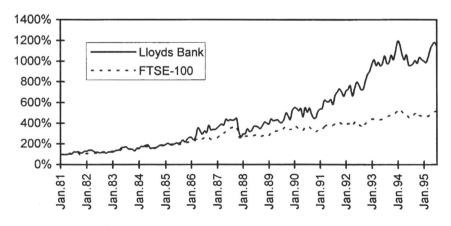

Figure 9.1   Relative stock price performance 1981–1995: Lloyds Bank
Source: Datastream

Moves by other banks in recent months to reduce their capital levels by buying back their shares (announcements by Citicorp on 20 June 1995 and by Barclays on 8 August 1995, for example) can also be seen as an application of the shareholder value concept, as will be seen later.

At Swiss Bank Corporation, putting the creation of shareholder value into the forefront of our way of thinking has caused some very profound changes. For example, all of our recent acquisitions (Brinson Partners, SG Warburg, various regional banks in Switzerland) have been funded out of retained earnings and/or subordinated debt, so as to increase the return available to shareholders. This departure from the accepted practice of maintaining very high capital ratios (especially in Switzerland) has been warmly welcomed by the stockmarket—SBC was the weakest performer amongst the 'Big Three' until the introduction of the new shareholder-focused strategy and structure at the beginning of 1994; since then, the stock has significantly outperformed the others. All of the acquisitions we have undertaken in this period were assessed on the basis of whether they create value for shareholders, and the Board is presented with periodical updates as to where we stand in terms of turning our performance into value, and where further work needs to be done. It should be emphasised that this pursuit of shareholder value is not single-minded, in that issues such as the bank's social role need to be given proper credit, but it is remarkable how problems can change when viewed under this new perspective.

Shareholder value analysis (SVA) is in essence no more than the application of the fundamental underlying principle of modern (i.e. post-war) finance: discounted cash flow. The value of any asset or investment is defined as the net present value of the expected cash flows, discounted using an interest rate which is set in relation to the riskiness of those cash flows. In addition to its initial application in the evaluation of investment projects within companies, the technique has been extended to the valuation of financial instruments such as bonds and stocks, and more recently derivatives. The SVA concept is nothing more than a further extension of the technique to the valuation of different strategic options within companies, so as to ensure that the maximum value is created for the shareholders.

Although Alfred Rappaport's 1986 textbook[1] is regarded as the first major textbook on the subject, the concept of maximising returns to shareholders is much older; indeed, it has been the fundamental objective of joint stock companies since their invention, although some seem to have lost their way since! The problem has been that the increasingly competitive, complicated and international marketplace has made it more and more difficult for managers to relate back to this basic goal, and they have lacked the tools to evaluate the impact of their actions. Rappaport provided the missing focus, and this has subsequently been refined into rigorous valuation methodologies, notably by Copeland *et al.* at McKinsey & Co.[2]

Table 9.1 illustrates one of the major implications of the SVA approach to valuing companies: even an apparently profitable business can actually destroy value. The example assumes a simple investment of $100, earning a 10% return over three years and recovering the initial investment at the end of the period.

In the first case, the investment is valued using a discount rate of 5%; as this is lower than the return generated (10%), value is successfully created: the present value of the investment is $113.6, against the starting value of $100. In the second case, the market value is calculated using a discount rate of 15%; the present value of $88.6 is lower than the starting value of $100, leading to a destruction of value.[3] If the shareholders require a return of 15%, the result will be a fall in the value of the company's stock, as a lower share price translates into a higher return. If this investment were an entire company, the value of the shares would fall from $100 to $88.6 at the outset, such that the return to shareholders over the period equals 15% per annum.

Although SVA is not directly linked to the measurement of capital *per se*, it plays a fundamental role in determining where capital is allocated, and thus an entire chapter is devoted here to the subject.

Table 9.1   Example of value creation and value destruction

Time	0	1	2	3
Equity	−100			
Revenue		10	10	110

$$\text{Market value (5\%)} = \frac{10}{1.05} + \frac{10}{1.05^2} + \frac{10}{1.05^3} = 113.6$$

$$\text{Market value (15\%)} = \frac{10}{1.15} + \frac{10}{1.15^2} + \frac{10}{1.15^3} = 88.6$$

SHARE BUY-BACKS AS AN APPLICATION OF SVA

The example given in Table 9.1 illustrates the problem seen in Chapter 1: increasing capital balances are tempting banks to make loans at cut-throat prices; even if the potential build-up of future loan loss write-offs is ignored, we now know that if the return on these loans is less than the cost of capital to the banks making the loans, then the share prices of the banks involved will suffer. In the preceding chapters, various ways of assessing the capital which is tied up in different investments have been examined (this is essential, as we cannot calculate the return if we do not know how much capital is invested!), and Chapters 5 and 6 introduced a method for assessing the appropriate cost of capital of individual businesses. Armed with these tools, managers can determine whether transactions, customers, businesses, divisions etc. are generating the necessary returns, the conclusion being that those which fall short require urgent management action (turnaround to reach the required hurdle rate, closure, or sale to a third party are the obvious choices).

Rather than investing in cut-price loans, banks faced with the problem of excess equity and not enough potential investments which generate the required level of return should attempt to repay the excess capital to the shareholders—such as by increasing dividends or by buying back their shares. This was the reason specifically given in the two recent buy-back announcements referred to above: Citicorp and Barclays. As reported in the press,[4] John Reed, Chairman of Citicorp, said that the bank 'was generating free capital in excess of that needed to fund our business'. Notably, the share price rose immediately after the announcement, which is precisely what one would expect from the example shown above, although admittedly not by a very dramatic amount. In the case of Barclays, the bank again gave 'accumulating capital too rapidly for its needs' as its reason, and the *Financial Times*[5] commented that this 'signalled a profound change of attitude . . . The idea that a UK bank will give back to shareholders capital for which it cannot find a good use has scarcely appeared credible until now'. The bank for the first time in over a decade seemed also to have given up its goal of being Britain's biggest bank, cutting back the loan portfolio and allowing National Westminster Bank to claim that dubious prestige. In the case of Barclays, the impact on the share price is difficult to establish, as the announcement coincided with the publication of the half-year results.

Share buy-backs have become quite commonplace in the US banking industry, and in the non-financial sector worldwide. It is now to be expected that the SVA focus is also adopted in the European financial sector, and further announcements of this sort can probably be expected, particularly where the growth in banks' profits outstrips the growth in their capital needs.

DIFFERENCE BETWEEN SVA AND EVA

Criticism is often levelled at the SVA concept for being too woolly; in particular, Rappaport's book is not very prescriptive when it comes to providing a framework for doing the actual valuations. A variant of SVA called economic value added (EVA) has been developed in recent years, and is finding increasing popularity as an 'alternative' to SVA. The principle of EVA is a rigorous calculation of the value created or destroyed over a particular period (called the 'economic profit'); the EVA for a period is usually defined as the change in the economic profit versus the previous period. Economic profit is essentially the profit earned over and above the cost of capital:

$$\text{Economic profit} = \text{NOPAT} - (\text{capital} \times k)$$

where NOPAT stands for net operating profit after tax and k refers to the cost of capital (usually the weighted average cost of capital, or WACC).

For example, an investment of $1000 returns a NOPAT of $350 over one year, and the cost of capital is 20%. The economic profit for the year is:

$$350 - (1000 \times 20\%) = \$150$$

Note that the $150 is a period-end value: it is the difference between the return earned and the required return, measured at the end of the period. The net present value of the investment is actually $125 ($150 discounted back over one year). Table 9.2 gives a multi-period example of an economic profit calculation, assuming a changing level of investment and changing returns over a three-year period; for each year, the economic profit is shown. The discount rate is 20%.

Note that in this example, the economic profit for the first year is negative, as the investment takes two years before it really starts to pay back. This is the main limitation of the EVA approach: as it is a single-period measure, it could potentially lead to value-adding investments being foregone. EVA is often touted as a good performance measurement tool, but

Table 9.2 Example of multi-period EVA calculation

	Year 1	Year 2	Year 3
Equity invested	1000	1200	1400
NOPAT	150	300	500
Economic profit	−50	60	220

in this example, the manager who made this investment has actually added value, as the overall returns exceed the cost of capital, but on a pure EVA basis, he would be penalised in year 1.

Fortunately, there is an approach which combines the precision of EVA with the overall goals of SVA: multi-period valuation as advocated by T. Copeland and his colleagues at McKinsey. Although critics of SVA attack its 'woolly' definitions, the McKinsey approach to valuation (which we still call SVA) is every bit as rigorous as EVA, if not more so. Under the McKinsey approach, the valuation of any business or invest-ment is defined as the net present value of the free cash flows generated by that business. Leaving aside for the moment the difference between 'free cash flow' and NOPAT, Table 9.3 shows that the SVA and EVA approaches are actually methodologically consistent ways of expressing the same thing in different ways.

Since the two methods apply the same discount rate to the same cash flows, it can be seen that the full valuation method (SVA) is equivalent to the net present value of the annual economic profit measures.

The differences between SVA and EVA can be summarised as follows:

1. SVA is future-oriented, and requires accurate rolling planning to produce a stream of expected cash flows. If used as a performance measure (change in

Table 9.3 Comparison of EVA and SVA measures (same example as Table 9.2)

Cash flows	Start	End of year 1	End of year 2	End of year 3	Total
Investment	−1000	−200	−200	1400	
NOPAT		150	300	500	
Net cash flow	−1000	−50	100	1900	
PV of cash flows	−1000	−42	69	1100	127
Econ. profit (Table 9.2)		−50	60	220	
PV of econ. profit		−42	42	127	127

SVA from one measurement point to the next) managers may be tempted to 'cheat' the SVA measure by making optimistic cash flow forecasts. (However, this can only be done for a short while, since before long the shortfall between the actual results and the optimistic plans is likely to lead to some searching questions). EVA on the other hand is based on actual performance (ex-post) for a particular period.

2. SVA is a multi-period measure, whereas EVA is a one-period measure. Just as managers can cheat SVA by making optimistic forecasts, they can cheat EVA by deferring investments. The examples in Tables 9.2 and 9.3 show clearly that a good investment can lead to negative EVA numbers in certain periods—just the kind of return to the bad old 'return-on-investment' days that Rappaport sought to relegate to the dustbin!

3. Most significantly, SVA uses free cash flow rather than NOPAT as the key measure. However, it is perfectly possible—even desirable—to calculate EVA based on free cash flow rather than NOPAT, just as in the above example SVA was calculated based on NOPAT.

'Free cash flow' means cash generated for the shareholders. The starting point is NOPAT, but then non-cash items from this (such as depreciation) are eliminated and the tax charge is re-stated based on cash outflow (elimination of deferred tax). From this amount of 'cash flow' any increase/decrease in the operating funding requirement of the business is deducted or added back: new investments, for example, or an increase/decrease in working capital. The result is 'free cash flow', which is available either for repayment to shareholders (such as in the form of dividends) or for reinvestment in new projects. If a firm generates net free cash flow, it will create value for its shareholders.

Note that whilst the rest of this chapter refers to the SVA full valuation approach, the issues raised in respect of assessing discount rates and defining free cash flow are equally valid for the EVA approach.

There are two major challenges in applying the SVA approach to banks: assessing the appropriate discount rate and defining/projecting free cash flow.

ASSESSING DISCOUNT RATES

The discount rate of a bank as a whole can be assessed by applying the capital asset pricing model: the additional cost of capital over the risk-free rate of a company (its risk premium) is proportional to its beta (ß), and the proportionality factor is the surplus return on the whole market over the risk-free rate, as seen in Chapter 5. The regression analysis on revenue volatility performed in that chapter is repeated in Table 9.4.

For example, given a risk-free rate of 5% and a market premium of

Table 9.4 Derivation of beta from revenue volatility

Std. dev. of annual revenues as % of average	Modelled beta
4	0.58
6	0.79
8	1.00
10	1.22
12	1.44
14	1.65
16	1.87
18	2.09
20	2.30

Based on the regression, beta = 0.14 + (10.82 × volatility).
The numbers in the table have been rounded slightly.

4%, the theoretical beta of a business whose annual revenue volatility (standard deviation as a percentage of the mean) is 10% can be determined as follows:

$$\beta = 0.14 + (10.82 \times 10\%) = 1.22$$
$$k_e = 5\% + (1.22 \times 4\%) = 9.9\%$$

This approach enables an evaluation of an appropriate discount rate not just for the whole bank, but also for alternative strategies and for individual businesses within the bank. It is very important that the interest rate used to discount earnings reflects the varying volatility (riskiness) of those earnings. For example, investments in relatively stable and predictable earnings—such as in a fee-driven business like private banking—may be discounted at fairly low rate (3%–4% over the risk free rate would not be untypical). A high-risk business, such as a very trading-oriented investment bank, would require a much higher discount rate— 10% or more above the risk-free rate. This can be seen from the price/earnings ratios of such institutions: whereas investment banks have ratios of around 7, those of private banks are often around 15–18.[6] If one simply discounts all expected cash flows at the bank's average cost of capital, investment in high-risk businesses will be encouraged at the expense of businesses with less risk. (To be very precise, when looking at strategic investments, one could use the regression approach to determine the discount rate, and hence the value, of the bank before and after the investment, and take the difference as the fair value of the investment).

Another point to be borne in mind is that the value of the cash flows of the bank as a whole may be different to the sum of the values of the individual businesses, as they are all discounted using different rates. The reason behind this is the diversification of earnings across different businesses, as discussed in Chapter 6. This difference can be positive or, more usually, negative, in which case one can talk of a 'conglomerate discount'. The values obtained through this process can be compared with the current stock market capitalisation (the market's assessment of the worth of the future cash flows), and with the target values the firm's management aspires to. Both Rappaport and Copeland have much to say on this, and how it can used to evaluate the strategic options available. In some cases, the conclusions (e.g. sell a profitable business) can be quite surprising.

Table 9.4 used a measure of the annual volatility to determine the appropriate beta. Since a time series of several years is not indicative of the riskiness of the business as it currently stands (as the business, regulatory and economic environment can change very significantly over such a long period), a monthly time series is more useful (24 months is probably a good balance between the need to be recent and the need to have enough data points in the distribution). The monthly values for the standard distribution are converted to annual values, as described in the statistical appendix to Chapter 4.

(Although Table 9.4 was used here and elsewhere to determine discount rates, this should not be regarded as an inviolable law of nature: it was based on a one-off analysis which was performed at SBC in support of an internal valuation methodology; one can easily question the banks used in the sample, the way in which 'outliers' were excluded, the time period over which the analysis was done etc., and it may well change over time. At SBC, we feel that it provides a good rule-of-thumb measure, and using revenue volatility as a driver of discount rates motivates managers to be more sensitive to the variance in their results during a period instead of just the period average.)

An alternative method is to use the dividend growth model to derive rates from market values. The dividend growth model says that the value of a share is equal to the expected next dividend, divided by a factor which covers both the discount rate (r) and a growth factor (g)—this is actually the formula for the present value of a growing perpetuity:

$$\text{Price} = \frac{D}{r - g}$$

Since the current market value of the stock is known, analyst's forecasts for the next dividend and for the expected growth rate can be used to determine the value of r. The drawbacks with this method are:

1. The values derived will change from day to day as the stock price changes, and in particular can be influenced by overall stock market sentiment. The CAPM model, on the other hand, uses long-term averages and is thus insensitive to short-term fluctuations.
2. Estimates for expected dividends may vary substantially from one analyst to another, and some analysts may not be clear in their assumptions as to growth rates.
3. Long-term growth rates must be assumed to be stable; particularly in start-ups, the values for g can be very high in the early years—if these are used blindly in the model, the value for $r-g$ can be very small or even negative, implying infinite value!
4. The model requires market prices and is difficult to apply to component businesses unless there are quoted specialist firms which engage only in that business which can be used to provide a benchmark.

DEFINITION OF FREE CASH FLOW

A forecast of future cash flows is needed in order to calculate the net present value. This gives rise to two challenges:

1. What is the definition of free cash flow?
2. How do we project this into the future (and thereby calculate the residual value at the end of the planning horizon)?

Definition of free cash flow

Free cash flow is the surplus or shortfall in cash flow generated by a business, having deducted any cash which needs to be reinvested. It is essentially the cash flow generated or absorbed in each period, representing either funds available to pay dividends (surplus) or an additional financing requirement (shortfall).The shareholder should be indifferent as to whether this free cash flow is paid out as a dividend or reinvested, as long as the incremental return is equal to his required return. If the incremental return is lower than the required return, the result will be a fall in the stock price as value is destroyed. Where companies can reinvest at rates higher than the required return, they create value for their shareholders, as the increased earnings generated will eventually be translated into dividends.

The normal way of calculating free cash flow for a non-financial company (the 'direct' method) is to adjust the P&L account by eliminating non-cash items such as depreciation, and then to add or deduct the cash flows which occur on the balance sheet—deduct investment in fixed assets, deduct/add any increase/reduction in external financing etc. Whilst technically feasible in the case of banks, this would involve being able to forecast the change in volume of all balance sheet positions—a notoriously difficult challenge. It is therefore easier to examine the net change in available equity as free cash flow (the 'indirect' method), as the sum of the changes in assets and liabilities must be equal to the change in shareholders' equity.

Whilst banks do not in general have a limit on how much external finance they can raise, they face a different constraint: the amount of dividend which a bank can pay is determined by the necessity to maintain a minimum amount of regulatory capital.

The following examples will help illustrate the point.

1. The bank lends $100 to a corporate client. Given an 8% capital requirement on corporate credits, the bank will finance $92 of the loan out of client funds or other liabilities, and $8 out of capital. The cost of financing $92 in liabilities is included in the bank's P&L account (i.e. already deducted from free cash flow), whereas as the additional capital requirement is not included in the P&L.
2. When a bank invests $100 in a new computer system, it may be required to match 50% of the investment out of capital and the rest is financed out of liabilities. As with the loan, only part of the cash outflow is included in the P&L account. In addition, the full investment will be written off over time against the P&L.

A possible first definition of free cash flow is therefore:

	Net profit after tax
plus	non-cash charges (depreciation)
minus	increase in the regulatory capital requirement

Note that credit provisions are treated as cash items in the indirect method: it is otherwise assumed that the cash lent out has been matched by cash borrowed (except for the capital requirement), and that on maturity the cash received back is repaid to the lenders. Once a default is incurred, the bank must repay the lenders, but receives less than the full amount of cash from the borrowers, and thus suffers a cash outflow. This effectively transfers the financing of the now dud loan from liabilities to capital (reflected by the loan loss charge-off to the P&L account, which reduced shareholders' equity), and is effective as soon as the provision is made, not on maturity of the loan.

Depreciation is treated as a non-cash item: nearly all assets ultimately have to be funded 100% out of equity, as the depreciation charged to the P&L account over time reduces equity. Thus 100% of investments are treated as negative free cash flow in the year the investment is made; any depreciation (a non-cash item) is added back to the profit each year.

This gives a revised definition of free cash flow, viz.:

	Net profit after tax
plus	non-cash charges (depreciation)
minus	increase in the regulatory capital requirement
minus	investment in fixed assets

However, there is a quirk in the capital requirements which needs to be taken into account: investment in fixed assets (buildings, equipment etc.) must also be backed by capital, for example by 50%. Since the full investment is charged against free cash flow, we need to ensure that we are not double-counting by also charging the increase in regulatory capital which relates to the investment in fixed assets.

Free cash flow is thus defined as:

	Net profit after tax
plus	non-cash charges (depreciation)
minus	increase in the regulatory capital requirement
minus	investment in fixed assets
plus	increase in regulatory capital requirement related to fixed assets

One can go even one step further, and distinguish fixed assets between depreciable items (such as computer installations) and non-depreciable items (such as freehold land). In such cases, there are two possible approaches: treat these in the same way as any normal business asset (no deduction of the investment from free cash flow, but the full change in regulatory capital reflected), or deduct them in full from free cash flow and then ignore the regulatory capital requirement altogether. The latter approach implicitly assumes that such assets are fully funded out of equity, even if the capital regulations allow an element of external financing (in Switzerland, for example, bank real estate needs to be matched with 20% of regulatory capital), and thus understates the free cash flow really available for shareholders.

The above definition uses regulatory capital; this can easily be replaced by any internal definition of capital, under the constraint that the internal capital measure for the bank as a whole cannot be lower than the minimum regulatory capital requirement.

Projected free cash flow

Many large companies demand 10-year forecasts from their divisional managers, as only over such a long period can sensible investment decisions be made. This sort of planning horizon is not common in banks, and in some cases could even be regarded as foolish (try forecasting investment banking revenues over 10 years!). In a typical SVA calculation of an ongoing business, around 75% of the total value will relate to cash flows occurring after the third year, and it is unusual for banks to forecast earnings for a longer period than this. The valuation is thus very susceptible to the choice of growth factor used in the valuation of the ongoing business (the 'residual value' in SVA parlance).

One approach is to use industry-wide historical growth factors to assess the potential future growth beyond the end of the planning horizon. Remember, however, that not only earnings growth, but also the growth rate for regulatory capital need to be forecast. A more conservative approach is to assume that after the end of the planning period, any incremental growth in earnings is matched by an incremental growth in capital requirements, or in other words that the return on the incremental capital is exactly equal to the cost of capital, and therefore has zero net present value. Growth rates can thus be ignored and the free cash flow of the final year of the planning horizon treated as a perpetuity.

The conservative approach is useful when using SVA as a simple performance measure, as it is the relative change in value from year to year which is important, not the absolute value. A more rigorous approach with either a longer planning period or some assumptions as to growth rates will need to be taken where the business being valued is not in a 'mature' state (for example, where the business is a start-up, where the valuation relates to a strategic acquisition where synergies might need to be realised over time, or where the business is in decline).

To determine growth factors, one can again use the dividend growth model seen above: this time we know r and can therefore calculate g (of course, this will not work where the dividend growth model was used in the first place to determine r, as we end up going round in circles!). Another approach is just to value the free cash flow of the final year of the planning period using industry-typical p/e's.

INTERPRETING THE RESULTS

Using this measurement tool encourages managers to either increase cash flow or decrease volatility, or both. It could be argued that the methodology outlined above simply encourages managers to make wildly optimistic plans for the future, so as to increase the cash flow used to measure the value of the business. However, this cannot be done continuously: having inflated cash flows in one planning cycle, the manager would have to inflate them by even more in the next planning cycle if he wanted to increase the apparent value. At some point, the difference between his plans and his budgets, and between his budgets and his actual results, is going to need some explanation. SVA is intentionally a management tool which only works in the medium- to long-term. It should encourage managers to extend their planning horizons and to forge a closer link between the paper plans and the execution of those plans. For the short-term, SVA needs to be supplemented by other measurements tools, such as EVA and an RoC measure.

When assessing strategies, managers need to ask themselves the following questions:

1. How would alternative strategies affect shareholder value?
2. Which strategy is likely to create the most value?
3. For the selected strategy, how sensitive is value to internal and external factors and assumptions?

In addition, the following questions have to be asked at group level:

1. Which businesses in the 'corporate portfolio' are creating the most value for shareholders?
2. Which businesses have limited value creation potential and are therefore candidates for potential divestiture?
3. Which combination of strategies will create the most total value?
4. Which businesses are cash generators and which are cash drains?
5. To what extent can the group fund its proposed strategy from internal cash flow, and how much additional capital has to be raised?

VALUING INDIVIDUAL BUSINESSES

Although the definition of free cash flow described above is applicable at all levels of the organisation, as one descends the organisational tree it is all too easy to become entangled in management accounting issues, such as transfer pricing and the allocation of central overheads (some of these issues were discussed in Chapter 7). There is no 'correct' answer to these issues—they must be resolved as part of the management philosophy of the bank. At SBC, we regard certain costs at group level as not being relevant to the individual divisions (such that the free cash flow of the group is less than the sum of the free cash flow of the divisions), and the same approach is taken again when going down within a division to the component businesses.

This organisational structure can lead to misallocation of capital if decisions are made at the wrong level in the hierarchy, as the example in Table 9.5 shows.[7]

Assume that the group only has $400 million available rather than the $600 million requested. If allocations are first made to divisions, then each division will receive $200 million since they are forecasting equal value creation. The divisions would then allocate internally to those businesses offering the best value creation; the resulting overall increase in value is shown in Table 9.6.

However, if capital is allocated directly to the businesses, value would be created as shown in Table 9.7.

The total value created by allocating directly to businesses is $35 million more than if capital is first allocated to divisions.

SVA AS A MEASURE OF SYNTHETIC EQUITY

One of the most interesting uses of SVA is its application in creating synthetic equity. For example, rather than paying all bonuses in cash, senior management may wish to defer part of the payment to ensure that managers and employees focus on a wider horizon than just the current year's bottom line (this helps to align objectives with those of the shareholders). In addition to simple bonus deferrals, some companies link the

Table 9.5 Result of making decisions at wrong level of hierarchy

	Division A (USD Mio's)		Division B (USD Mio's)	
Business	Capital requested	Value created	Capital requested	Value created
1	100	130	100	50
2	100	15	100	50
3	100	5	100	50
	300	150	300	150

Table 9.6 Allocation to divisions first

	Capital allocated	Value created
Division A		
Business 1	100	130
Business 2	100	15
Division B		
Business 1	100	50
Business 2	100	50
Total	400	245

value of the deferred bonus with performance over the deferral period. Most easily, this is done by indexing the deferred bonus to the firm's stock (preferably to the *relative* performance of the stock to the market as a whole, to eliminate the effects of overall market moves). In some cases, the deferral simply represents the granting of stock or stock options with a minimum retention period before the stock can be sold or the option exercised. A simpler alternative is to make the cash bonus payout each year dependent or partly dependent on the change in value of the company or divisions over the past year, although the loss of a 'lock-in' mechanism (deferred bonuses are usually forfeited if the employee resigns during the deferral period) might make this less desirable than a deferred bonus scheme.

Whereas it might be sensible to link the bonuses of senior management to the performance of the bank as a whole, it might be more difficult to persuade more junior managers that their hard-earned cash is

Table 9.7 Allocations direct to businesses

	Capital allocated	Value created
Division A		
Business 1	100	130
Division B		
Business 1	100	50
Business 2	100	50
Business 3	100	50
Total	400	280

going to be invested in something over which they have little or no control. Thus the managers of division A are going to be bitterly disappointed if the stock price performs badly as a result of poor performance in division B, and would prefer to have the bonus linked to the performance of their own division.

SVA valuations can be used to support this by creating a synthetic stock in each division; the value of the 'stock' is based on the valuation of the division at a point in time. The valuations are repeated at regular intervals (e.g. semi-annually or annually) and the change in value can be treated as a change in the value of the 'stock' and the deferred bonus adjusted accordingly. EVA can also be used to achieve this, with the deferred bonus pool adjusted upwards or downwards accordingly at the end of each year, depending on the EVA measure. Companies may make the performance totally dependent on the synthetic stock, or dependent on a mixture of actual group stock, divisional synthetic stock and cash (invested at the risk-free rate). The performance can either be linearly linked (where the bonus pool is exposed to both upside as well as downside, although in the current climate it is difficult to imagine staff accepting bonus deferrals which could significantly deteriorate in value before payout) or with option-like features (such as a call on the synthetic stock, preferably capped to prevent virtually free enjoyment of the upside with little or no downside).

It was mentioned above that the danger with both SVA and EVA measures is their susceptibility to management manipulation. This obviously becomes even more acute when a good portion of managers' personal wealth is dependent on such a measure. It is therefore very important to ensure that sufficient safeguards are established to prevent this. It is recommended that the following three features be an integral part of any EVA or SVA performance measurement system:

1. Business plans used to provide input to valuations should be subject to very rigorous scrutiny and aggressive debate at board level. The result of this process should be a business plan on which all managers can sign off.
2. The period over which bonuses are deferred should be sufficiently long to ensure that the negative consequences of any manipulation (suppression of necessary investments in EVA, over-optimistic planning in SVA) come to light and impact current performance measures before the deferral is released for payment.
3. The calculations must be performed or reviewed by an independent, sufficiently qualified unit. The management accounts on which calculations might be based must be of high quality and reconcilable to audited financial statements.

SUMMARY

An understanding of how value is created and how it is destroyed is fundamental to ensuring that capital is allocated in the most efficient way possible. Investing in businesses which fail to earn their cost of capital will eventually destroy value, whereas investing in businesses which generate returns in excess of the cost of capital creates value for shareholders. It is important also to recognise that the cost of capital is different for different businesses, depending on the degree of risk involved in their returns; using a single cost of capital (the discount factor in the NPV calculation) will result in low-risk businesses being starved of capital whilst the more volatile businesses benefit. It is also important to realise that the measurement perspective must extend beyond one year to ensure that managers are not encouraged to defer needed investment.

The primary difference between the SVA approach and the RoC approach discussed elsewhere in this book is the fact that the SVA approach is not a single-period model, but takes into account the possibility of investing to earn more in the future. The ultimate test of the effectiveness of any bank's capital allocation system must be whether it is capable of ensuring that value is created for shareholders, and it must therefore send out the right signals to managers in terms of how their performance is assessed. The way in which capital allocation can be used as a 'corporate language' for sending out the right signals to managers and staff is the subject of the next, final, chapter.

ENDNOTES

1. Alfred Rappaport, *Creating Shareholder Value: The new standard for business performance*, The Free press, NY, 1986.
2. Valuation: Measuring and Managing the Value of Companies, T. Copeland, T. Koller and J. Murrin (McKinsey & Co), John Wiley & Sons Inc, NY, 1994 (second edition).
3. My thanks to Prof. Jean Dermine of INSEAD for this example.
4. *Financial Times*, 21 June 1995
5. *Financial Times*, 9 August 1995
6. One standard method of valuing stocks is the dividend growth model, which discounts expected dividends by a discount factor adjusted for future growth:

$$\text{Price} = \frac{D}{r - g}$$

In an extreme case of no growth, the earnings each year are paid out as a dividend, and earnings are equal to dividends. In such cases, g is 0 and the model is simply earnings divided by the discount factor. Expressed differently, the p/e ratio is the inverse of the discount rate, and a p/e of 7 implies a discount rate of c.14% whereas a p/e of 15 implies a rate of c. 7%.

7.   Taken from Rappaport, p. 105 (see Note 1).

Implementing Capital Allocation Policies and Procedures: Moving from a Passive System to an Active One

This final chapter looks beyond the mainly technical issues covered so far, and examines the managerial aspects of implementing a capital allocation system. The typical stages in the development of such a system and the options available are examined first; this is followed by a look at the process itself and its implementation. The chapter concludes with a discussion of the kind of barriers to implementation which exist. As in earlier chapters, the generic term 'RoC' is used to refer to any measure of performance which divides some definition of 'return' (profit, contribution, revenue etc., where non-accounting items such as risk costs and cost of capital may form part of the definition) by some definition of 'capital' (regulatory capital, risk capital etc.).

CAPITAL ALLOCATION AS A PERFORMANCE MEASURE

A performance measure which cannot be influenced by the behaviour of those being measured is of little use, as it will have no incentive effect. Indeed, one of the most difficult and dangerous aspects of any performance measurement system is what the author likes to call the 'Heisenberg principle of MIS', after the German scientist Werner Heisenberg, one of the founders of quantum mechanics. Heisenberg's famous uncertainty principle is related to the problem of observing the exact speed and location of particles: this can only be done by shining light or some other wave on the particles, which has the effect of changing the path and/or velocity of the particle being measured. The more precise the measurement, the shorter the wavelength required and the higher the energy transmitted. Thus the more precise one wishes to be about the particle's location, the less precise one can be about the particle's path. The same problem occurs in any performance measurement system: the act of measuring performance will influence the person being measured to change his behaviour, possibly in a way which is detrimental to the interests of the institution. Indeed, one commentator of performance-related incentive schemes has even observed that 'Do rewards motivate people? Absolutely. They motivate people to get rewards'.[1] Properly designed performance measures must be linked to actionable goals which are consistent with the overall strategy of the bank, to avoid motivating behaviour which is contrary to that strategy.

The criteria for a successful performance measure are:

1. It must be transparent (easily understood).
2. It must be practicable (calculated without undue effort).
3. It must be actionable (managers can influence the outcome).
4. It must be consistent with the strategic goals of the bank.

It is against these criteria that the effectiveness of various capital allocation techniques must be judged.

STAGES IN THE DEVELOPMENT OF A CAPITAL ALLOCATION PROCESS

Capital allocation processes can be divided into two classes: a 'passive' approach and an 'active' approach. Under the 'passive' heading are grouped all capital allocation processes which derive an amount of capital attributable to a bank as a whole or to a particular business, transaction etc., but which do not attempt to steer this number. In its simplest form, this can be the statement of regulatory capital requirements submitted by a bank to its supervisor. This might be further supplemented by an alternative definition of capital, such as risk capital, and may be broken down by business units. A further stage in the evolution of the process might be the application of the imputed capital in a performance-measurement context.

An 'active' approach to capital allocation uses the process to influence business results: adjusting the capital allocated to particular businesses and encouraging managers to maximise returns on this allocated capital. By this means, the management of the bank can adjust, for example, the risk capital available to businesses.

The switch from a passive approach to an active one is dependent on the capital allocation methodology being accepted by managers as a formal part of the performance measurement process. Without this, the imputation of capital to a business remains an academic exercise—business heads will not feel bound by the imputed capital, and any attempt to steer the performance of the bank by changing the allocation will have no impact.

Two steps in the transition from a passive to an active approach can be envisaged: firstly, the calculations are broadly circulated and discussed, and management's acceptance of the methodology is gained. This can be done, for example, by stating broad return expectations as part of the planning process. In a second step, the imputed RoC (or risk-adjusted measure) becomes a formal component of the performance-related compensation of business managers, and perhaps even at lower levels within the organisational hierarchy. The bank is now able to take a more active role in capital allocation decisions, and the link to performance-measurement ensures that business managers have an incentive to maximise the return on the resources given to them. These steps are summarised in Figure 10.1.

Most banks are currently probably somewhere between the purely passive and semi-active stages, perhaps starting to link the capital measure with performance measurement, with a very few banks already adopting a full active approach to capital allocation.

WHAT KINDS OF CAPITAL ALLOCATION MEASURES EXIST?

The capital allocation techniques covered by this book can be grouped under three main headings:

- regulatory capital requirements (Chapter 3);
- asset-volatility-based   risk-adjusted-performance   measures—RAPM—Chapter 4), with virtually endless varieties in both the definition of capital and the RoC formula;
- earnings-volatility-based RAPM (Chapter 6), again with virtually endless varieties in both the definition of capital and the RoC formula.

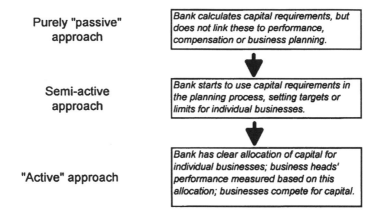

Figure 10.1   Typical stages in the development of a capital allocation
methodology

This book has concentrated on these approaches, as they are the most widespread and are generally supported by a rigorous theoretical framework. To be comprehensive, however, the following additional definitions of the capital employed in a particular business should be considered; these can be described as 'economic' capital approaches:

1. *Benchmark capital* – meaning the paid-in capital which a business would require if it were an independent legal entity with no backing from a parent company. In no case can this be less than the legal minimum (i.e. the regulatory capital), as it would not be possible to operate below this threshold. It may however be much higher than the legal minimum—private banks, for example, have extremely high capital ratios, even though they have little in the way of regulatory capital requirements. They also have very stable earnings and need little risk capital: the reason behind the high capital ratios is simply that the high net worth individuals who make up their client base wish to deposit their savings in a very safe bank. This measure of capital is usually obtained by benchmarking against banks which specialise in the relevant field—for example, the average capital expressed as a percentage of total assets under management may be ascertained for a group of private banks, and then applied as an internal capital ratio to a banking group's own private banking business.

2. *Stress scenarios* – meaning the worst-case loss in value which a bank could incur. This can be assessed by looking at the different risk classes and determining appropriate stress scenarios for each. At SBC, for example, we have a stress test limit system for our trading portfolios, involving potential crash-type scenarios. We measure the 'stress test' market risk capital as the sum of the utilisation of these limits (i.e. assuming that all stress events occur simultaneously). For credit risks, we assume that all statistical default rates used in the measurement of expected losses (as described in Chapter 7)

move up by two standard deviations against their historical average (again, all at the same time). We assume that all legal cases in which the bank faces a potential loss are decided against the bank, and that the bank's own real estate (branch network) falls in value by a certain percentage. The sum of all these and other possible disasters equals the stress test capital, which can be compared to the available equity of the bank to see how much 'cover' is maintained (the available capital of the bank expressed as a multiple of the stress-test capital).

3. *Insurance/hedging costs* – As discussed briefly in Chapter 6, the capital available to a bank can be thought of as a kind of insurance against deterioration in value of the assets.[2] If one can come up with a measure of the cost of insuring those assets, or hedging them, then one can derive a surrogate measure of capital. For some credit products, the premium which the market requires over the risk-free rate for securitised assets (mortgage-backed securities, credit card receivables etc.) might be a good guide to the insurance cost—any guarantees given may have to be separately priced, which is really only feasible if a third party has provided the guarantee for a fee.

All of these definitions of economic capital—and any others which the creative reader may care to dream up—can be useful, and it is not recommended that banks select just one at the expense of all others, as each has its uses in different contexts. The benchmark capital approach, for example, is the only feasible approach for a business—such as private banking—which cannot be subsumed under a more rigorous statistical approach; it can also be useful when trying to establish how much of the firm's risk and/or regulatory capital should be allocated to a particular business (under-allocation of capital can starve a potentially profitable business, and over-allocation has the equally dangerous effect of fuelling unwanted risk-taking or of subsidising growth in unprofitable businesses). Observing the capital levels of benchmark specialist banks is a good way of ensuring that the in-house model is producing meaningful results. The stress scenario approach is useful as a comparison against regulatory capital—for example, these sort of calculations have recently been used to demonstrate to the Basle Committee that the proposed parameters for market risk capital greatly exceed even the worst crash scenarios of the past ten years.[3]

SELECTION AND IMPLEMENTATION OF A CAPITAL ALLOCATION MODEL

When selecting which model to adopt, management needs to consider more than just the technical issues (which model appears, on paper, to be the most appropriate). The following issues will also need to be addressed:

1. *The major challenges which face the bank* – Thus a bank which is faced with a shortage of regulatory capital may need to give this prominence, perhaps even starting out with a pure return-on-regulatory-capital. Where the bank is more concerned with the volatility of its earnings, then either the revenue-volatility or asset-volatility approach may be the most appropriate.

2. *Gathering the necessary data* – The statistical modelling required by many approaches is only one aspect of the implementation—most modern PCs can handle this with ease, and the mathematics involved is widely taught at universities. A much bigger challenge is obtaining the in-house data required—distributions of daily revenues, for example, or the sensitivity of a portfolio to movements in underlying financial markets. Trying to do this centrally in a large, international organisation is bound to fail: it is much more advisable to have an agreed-upon methodology, with calculations at the detail level (transactions, customers etc.) done non-centrally. Given that senior management does not usually need to 'drill down' to the level of individual transactions, the bank-wide calculations can be performed periodically, based on summary data provided by non-central units.

3. *Signals management wishes to send* – The 'Heisenberg principle' of management information was referred to earlier: managers will align their performance to maximise whatever performance measures are imposed on them. It is therefore very important to think through the consequences of different performance measurement models, perhaps with someone playing the role of devil's advocate, trying to find ways to arbitrage the system to produce fictitiously good performance metrics (such as in the problems related to NPV accounting and single-period RoC numbers which were examined in Chapter 7).

There are also a number of prerequisites which would seem essential to the proper implementation of a capital-based performance measure:

1. *Senior management commitment* – Banks which have successfully focused on improving return on capital show a very strong commitment from senior management: the development of RAROC at Bankers Trust under CEO Charles Sanford, or Brian Pitman's disciplined focus on RoC at Lloyds Bank are the two most obvious examples. Without this commitment, the signals sent from the top will be confusing, and business heads will not have a clear incentive to push the philosophy down the line.

2. *Communication and education* – The effort required to school business people in the proposed measurement tool must not be underestimated. Many front-line managers (justifiably) take a cynical view of the latest fad coming out of head office, and yet it is critical to gain their acceptance of the methodology, which will otherwise remain a paper exercise with no impact on business results.

3. *Maintaining integrity over the process* – It is clearly beneficial to have front-line people involved in the development of the process—this guaran-

tees their acceptance of it—but at the same time management needs to be wary of granting a blank cheque. Where calculations are performed non-centrally, controls need to be in place to ensure that they are performed properly and professionally.

Typically, a central function (such as financial control or risk control) might be charged with the task of designing an appropriate model and agreeing the details with line managers. This unit will then also be responsible for the initial training, perhaps concentrating on the non-central financial control people, who can then cascade the education process down through the organisation. The central unit will also be responsible for performing the calculations at a consolidated level, and for ensuring the integrity of the process (ensuring numbers balance through to management accounts which are known to be reliable, for example).

WHAT APPROACHES COULD BE USED TO LINK CAPITAL ALLOCATION WITH PERFORMANCE?

Having come up with a broad definition of capital (or perhaps several different definitions), the next step in moving from a passive capital allocation system to an active one will be to link the capital allocation measure to the performance measurement model. As one might expect from the wide variety of potential capital allocation models to choose from, there are also a number of different capital-based performance measures, with an almost unlimited number of intermediate flavours, depending on the exact definition of 'return' and 'capital' in each case.

1. *Single-period RoC models* – Although these have many shortcomings, this sort of approach will in many cases be the first step in linking capital allocation to performance measurement. The major problem with this kind of performance model is that it focuses entirely on single-period returns—excessive bonuses may be paid in good years, and the short-term focus may encourage managers to defer necessary investment so as to maximise the current year's apparent performance. Some compensation experts have noted that traders' bonuses are in the form of a free call option: big bonuses are paid when big profits are made, but there is no downside risk if profits are not made (other than the foregoing of more bonuses). This may encourage traders to take excessive risks, as they can only win if the bet pays off. A first step in defusing

this situation is to make the RoC performance-related model based on some definition of risk capital.

2. *Single-period RoC models with multi-period bonus retention* – Many firms are currently moving towards this approach, under which bonuses are linked to an RoC performance measure, and then a portion of the bonus is deferred for a fixed period of time before it is released for payment (e.g. for three years). If the employee leaves the firm in the interim, he/she usually forfeits any deferred bonuses. The deferred bonus usually attracts interest. This approach has the advantage of encouraging loyalty, with the (weak) motivation factor that people who stay with the firm will want to earn future bonuses, and are therefore less likely to maximise current-year performance at the expense of future years.

3. *Single-period RoC models with RoC-model-related multi-period bonus retention* – This is a variation on the deferral model, whereby the deferred bonus can be 'topped up' by a factor related to performance during the deferral period. This ensures a stronger link between current and future year performance.

4. *Multi-period RoC models* – Whilst the author is not aware of any institution which measures performance on this basis, it is perfectly conceivable that the current year's bonus be based on a performance measure covering a longer period, such as a rolling average RoC over the past three years; this would encourage steady performance over time. The main problem with such a model is simply the market: bonuses would not be so high in good years as at other institutions with single-period models, as the good years are averaged with other years. Although bonuses would be higher in the reverse situation—as performance in bad years is ameliorated through the averaging with better years—bank employees, particularly in the trading room, are not known for their long-term loyalty and may in good years be tempted away to other firms.

5. *EVA and SVA models* – Two variations are conceivable here—a performance measure which is itself based on EVA or change in SVA, or a bonus deferral which is linked to synthetic stock (as we saw in the previous chapter), or even both. The commonest form of this approach is to pay bonuses, or at least a portion thereof, in the form of stock which must be held for a minimum period. This type of model provides the best incentives to maximise multi-period returns and ensures that employees are motivated to do what management is trying to do—maximise shareholder value. The disadvantage (in the eyes of the employ-

ees) is that the value of the deferred bonuses can go down as well as up, and it is questionable whether such a model could be imposed in an employment market where most banks still use single-period measures (Salomon Brothers reportedly tried to implement such a scheme at the end of 1994 and had to abandon it several months later in the face of employee dissatisfaction and defections). However, it remains the opinion of the author that bonus deferrals linked to the value of the firm (or division within a firm) will need to become the norm over the next decade to ensure that the interests of shareholders, managers and employees are better aligned.

The emphasis with all of these models is on positive encouragement to maximise return, not on a system of penalties if capital limits are transgressed. This is because a 'negative' system of capital 'limits' gives no incentive to improve returns, or to use less than the allotted amount of capital. A 'positive' system, based on RoC, however, encourages managers to maximise returns and not to utilise any unwanted capital if it does not produce the required returns.

However, where a bank is faced with a tight constraint on its capital —for example, where the competing bids for capital exceed the available capital—management may need to consider two variations to the RoC measure, which can be used individually or in combination:

1. Treat the denominator in the equation as being the higher of utilised capital or allocated capital; this has the effect of motivating businesses not to 'bid' for capital which is then not utilised (which could otherwise be allocated to other businesses):

$$\frac{\text{return}}{\text{max [utilised capital; allocated capital]}}$$

2. Charge the cost of any excess capital over the allotted amount at a punitive rate against return; this ensures that businesses do not 'grab' capital which has been allotted to another business:

$$\frac{\text{return} - (\text{excess capital} \times \text{punitive rate})}{\text{utilised capital}}$$

3. In combination, the denominator of the RoC equation would always use allocated capital and any excess over the allocated amount would be charged against the return. Thus any unused capital hits the

denominator and any over-utilisation hits the numerator; leaving the first of the above two options unchanged would result in any over-utilisation of capital on both sides of the fraction.

$$\frac{\text{return} - (\text{excess capital} \times \text{punitive rate})}{\text{allocated capital}}$$

A DYNAMIC CAPITAL ALLOCATION PROCESS

Having established a system of capital-based performance measures and linked these to compensation, the bank is now in a position to build a dynamic capital allocation process, as shown in Figure 10.2.

The first step in the process is to determine the capital available for allocation. This may simply be the available regulatory capital, but is preferably a more sophisticated calculation, taking into account the risk appetite of the organisation and determining the amount of risk capital management wishes to make available (the model demonstrated in Chapter 5 can be used to achieve this).

Having established the amount of capital available, it is important to

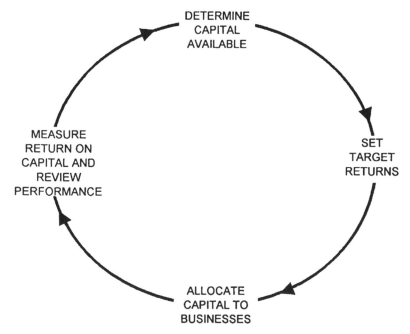

Figure 10.2   Dynamic capital allocation process

set targets for the sort of returns which management expects. These targets may be different for different businesses: different levels of risk will require different hurdle rates (the riskier the earnings stream, the higher the required return must be), and management may also wish to invest in strategic projects (such as new businesses) which will not yet generate the required return. It may also be desirable to maintain a certain level of diversification across businesses, even if some of these are not as profitable as others.

In a third step, management will allocate capital to businesses. This is an incremental process—capital already committed to a business cannot be withdrawn overnight (for example, the existing engagements with clients will continue to employ capital until they expire). Thus the capital allocation process consists of a series of 'fine tuning' over time—businesses which are employing too much capital will be given slightly less, forcing the business managers to reduce the number of new engagements entered into as old engagements mature, whereas businesses which are to be built up will gradually receive more capital.

The fourth step in the allocation loop is to measure the performance generated on the capital employed. This in turn provides input to the next round of allocation, as management adjusts its expectations and thus the amount of capital allocated to each business. Typically, the allocation process will be performed annually, as part of the bank's planning/budgeting cycle (at SBC, we combine a three-year planning horizon with a one-year, more detailed, budget. Capital is allocated annually, with the rolling three-year plan enabling management to steer longer-term investment and set expectations well in advance).

The performance measurement itself will usually be more frequent than the capital allocation process—it should be an integral part of the bank's internal management reporting (quarterly, monthly, or even weekly/daily for trading activities). The periodic performance measurement needs to focus on the RoC numbers generated, to ensure that the bank is constantly working towards its stated goals. In extreme cases, management may need to re-adjust the capital allocation during the year, for example where business performance significantly deviates from expectations. At SBC, in addition to the regular monthly management information which includes (annualised) RoC metrics, we also produce detailed quarterly analyses which cover such questions as:

1. How much capital do we currently have available?
2. How much capital are we currently utilising?
3. What is our forecast availability and usage over the coming quarters? (particularly important when management are contemplating acquisitions).

4. What returns have we earned on the capital allocated?
5. What changes in capital allocation do we recommend?

The analyses cover more than one definition of capital (regulatory capital and risk capital are the two standards; these are supplemented by other definitions on an *ad hoc* basis to support strategic decisions).

BARRIERS TO IMPLEMENTATION

Despite the high level of interest which this topic has generated, very few banks (especially outside the USA) have implemented any sort of internal risk-adjusted capital allocation process; why is this? There have been very few public studies as to how far banks have got with implementing RAPM, and those that have been published may not be fully up to date, and so it is difficult to give precise answers to this question. There is some evidence that a large number of banks have tried and failed to implement some sort of risk-based capital system; the 1993 study by Salomon Brothers[4] research department concluded: 'For every bank like Bankers Trust, which has successfully introduced a bankwide risk evaluation framework, there are many more which have failed because of the complexity of the formula, lack of management commitment and the resistance of traditional managers.'

The obstacles to implementation can be grouped under two headings: technical and cultural.

TECHNICAL OBSTACLES TO IMPLEMENTATION

Unclear measurement of 'return'

Most of this book has concentrated on the various possible definitions of 'C' (capital) in the 'RoC' equation, although Chapter 7 addressed some key issues relating to the definition of 'return'. Whichever definition is taken, it is very important to ensure that there is a reliable, stable source of management information on which to base the calculations. Once managers start to question the validity of the earnings attributed to them, the value of the performance measurement process naturally deteriorates very quickly. Things which can cause problems here include:

1. Constant changes in the definition of revenue (are statistical credit costs a deduction from revenue or a provision?) and of contribution (after direct costs only, or including allocations? Allocated on what basis?). As organi-

sations move away from financial accounts of legal entities to functional structures with different business sharing a common infrastructure, there is a big danger of a babel of different reports, each purporting to show the 'true' picture produced by each business. At SBC, one of the first things we did when establishing the new, functionally-driven structure, was to define a basic and clearly defined framework for reporting performance. Businesses are free to go into a greater level of detail within this structure, but cannot change the overall framework or the meaning of its components. Thus, for example, there is a common definition of what is, and what is not, included in 'net revenue'.

2. Unclear or shifting transfer pricing policies between the businesses. As with the clear definition of 'revenue', 'direct cost' etc., it is very important that all of the revenues, costs etc., of the organisation be clearly delegated to individual businesses. These businesses should be free to organise themselves as they wish, but the demarcation between the businesses needs to be stable and clearly defined.

3. Changes in the organisation itself. These are unavoidable, but it is very difficult to make comparisons over time if the organisation, division etc. being compared is itself changing, such as through acquisition of new businesses or closure of existing ones. It is thus advisable to keep management accounting data at a detailed level, and to store this over time. For example, a business may consist of several departments, but senior management may only look at the business as a whole. Where a single department is closed, or transferred to another business, it is easier to restate the previous performance of the whole business based on the new organisation if the single department can be eliminated from the time series.

Metric based on factors which are outside the control of the managers

A purely passive approach to capital allocation—as described above—will not be as successful as a more active approach, i.e. one in which the capital allocation process is an integral part of the way in which performance is measured and compensated. Whilst it might be necessary to introduce the concept on a passive basis, if the switch to active is left for too long, the whole effort will be wasted on what becomes a solely academic exercise. The issue of 'influence' goes in both directions—managers must be able to influence the outcome, and the outcome must have some influence on the performance assessment of managers.

Choosing the right components in the model plays a critical role here. For example, the definition of 'return' in 'return on capital' could be based on revenues, contribution, net profit, etc. Most measures of net profit include a number of items which are outside the control of the business managers (head office overhead, taxes etc.), and they may not be fully motivated if their performance is based on this number. Likewise, most cost allocations—even of relatively 'direct' costs—include an arbitrary element, and managers may spend more time trying to question the cost allocation than managing the capital allocated to them.

The same problem can be incurred when basing risk capital on the volatility of earnings—if only gross earnings are used, for example, then many important items like loan loss provisions may not be included. On the other hand, basing the metric on the volatility of net profit is not going to be successful, as this number contains many indirect items and may anyway be subject to a level of uncontrollable volatility (such as corrections to cost accruals from one period to the next).

Picking a model which is not appropriate for the organisation

This problem is determined by the degree of homogeneity or complexity of the component businesses: forcing a commercial credit business into a value-at-risk model designed primarily for the trading room, for instance, will simply result in meaningless numbers. In a complex, multi-business organisation a generic model (such as one based on earnings volatility) may be needed for all businesses, with each business looking individually at the drivers of that volatility and implementing its own bottom-up model accordingly. At a consolidated (total business) level, the two metrics should match (to within a reasonable degree).

Statistical overkill

With asset-volatility-based models, and also to a lesser extent with earnings-volatility-based ones, there is a big danger of statistical overkill. A degree of statistical sophistication is necessary, but beyond a certain level there are two problems which can be encountered:

1. The model becomes too complicated for anyone other than a small group of insiders to understand, and thus will be treated with suspicion.
2. Users forget that the model is just that—an attempt to explain approximately what happens in reality. There are so many assumptions and simplifications built into these kind of models that the accuracy of the results can be spurious.

CULTURAL OBSTACLES TO IMPLEMENTATION

As noted, there is very little in the way of published research on the status of RAPM implementation in banks; the following hypotheses are suggested by the author's own experiences, both within SBC and from attending conferences on the subject.

1. 'Where's the problem?' Many bankers have spent their careers in a well-protected industry, where the demands of the shareholders were not always high up on the agenda. Banks may encounter difficulties in persuading managers that capital is a scarce resource and that there is a need to generate adequate returns.
2. 'Not on my patch.' Having gained acceptance that capital is a scarce resource, banks may still encounter problems persuading managers to give up their fiefdoms—under RAPM, some businesses may no longer look attractive. For example, under most measures, commercial lending (especially international lending) is not profitable enough to cover the risks. Whilst banks may want to stay in the business so as to keep the customer relationship and cross-sell more profitable products, the loan officer is not going to willingly give up his traditional role as one of the most powerful people in the bank.
3. 'Its a technical thing.' Senior management needs to understand that they must lead the organisation by setting the performance measurement criteria and making their support very public. The introduction of an internal capital allocation system affects the whole philosophy of the bank, and management must be prepared to push it through. Very often, this may mean making unpleasant decisions.
4. 'Rap who?' Education is critical: if the capital allocation model remains a head office tool only, there will be very little benefit to the organisation. It must be broadly understood, accepted and used throughout the organisation to ensure that employees and senior management are working towards the same goals.
5. 'How much?!!' The complexity required of sophisticated, bankwide system such as Bankers Trust's RAROC is expensive, both in terms of computer hard- and software, as well as the salaries of the experts required to build the system. Throw in an external firm of consultants and it starts to get very expensive indeed. A more successful route to implementation is to start with a simple, high-level approach (such as the earnings-volatility approach described in Chapter 6) and then gradually improve on it. This will enable a better alignment of the investment in the system with the gradual acceptance thereof by line managers, and gives plenty of opportunity to correct at an early stage what would otherwise be very expensive mistakes.

Where RAPM has been successfully introduced—and again we have to cite Bankers Trust as the prime example—the single most important factor in getting the concept implemented has been the commitment of senior management.

SUMMARY

Whilst efficient capital allocation does not guarantee success, failure to make the best returns possible on the resources invested by shareholders will almost certainly guarantee sub-optimal performance in an increasingly competitive market. Allocating capital even on a relatively rudimentary basis—such as capital adequacy regulations—goes a long way to improving the efficiency of the resource utilisation.

The capital allocation methodology used can be drawn from a pool of available models. The earnings-volatility approach is the easiest to implement and communicate, but only works well at a high degree of aggregation (e.g. whole businesses). The asset-volatility approach, on the other hand, works very well even at the level of individual transactions, but is very costly to implement, and difficult (if not impossible) to integrate across heterogeneous businesses.

When choosing a model, management must not lose sight of the practicalities – all too often, the RAPM initiative dies away as a small group of technicians works on statistical models which are beyond the comprehension of those who are to use them. An iterative, evolutionary approach is preferable to a 'big bang' approach, as it allows the organisation to learn in parallel with the development of the process. A simple model introduced and accepted can be subsequently enhanced, whereas a complex model introduced in one go will meet a much higher level of resistance due to the lack of understanding.

Coupling the capital allocation process with a capital-based performance metric which is understandable, practicable and actionable—and linking compensation to this metric—will provide the link between incentives for management and the overall strategic goals of the bank. Whatever the details of the strategy, the increasingly competitive investment marketplace requires that shareholder value be in the forefront. It is impossible to forecast what the banking world will look like ten or twenty years from now, but as banks are faced with new competitors from outside their national borders as well from outside their traditional industry, as the banking industry continues to be convulsed with mergers and the existing over-capacity gets weeded out of the system, it is safe to bet that the banks which, looking back over this period, appear to investors of the future to have provided the best returns will be those banks which understand now that they need to utilise their capital more efficiently, and which act decisively to ensure that this happens.

ENDNOTES

1. Alfie Kohn, 'Why incentive plans cannot work', *Harvard Business Review*, September–October 1993, pp. 54–62.
2. Robert C. Merton and André F. Perold, 'Management of risk capital in financial firms', in *Financial Services: Perspectives and Challenges*, ed. Samuel L. Hayes, Harvard Business School Press, 1993.
3. Response by the International Swaps and Derivatives Association (ISDA) to the Basle Committee's market risk proposals, July 1995, as reported in the *Financial Times* on 4 August 1995.
4. *Capital in Banking and Insurance*, Salomon Brothers, New York, April 1993.

Index